Dear Ava,
      I hope you have fun making
some of these recipes.
                  Love you,
                  Grammie

THE
COMPLETE COOKBOOK
FOR TEENS

The Complete Cookbook for TEENS

120+ RECIPES TO LEVEL UP YOUR KITCHEN GAME

JULEE MORRISON

ROCKRIDGE
PRESS

Interior and Cover Designer: Suzanne LaGasa
Art Producer: Janice Ackerman
Editor: Marjorie DeWitt
Production Editor: Matt Burnett

Photography: © 2020 Marija Vidal. Food Styling by Victoria Woollard.

p. v: top: Elysa Weitala, bottom: New Africa/shutterstock; p. x, p. 8: Darren Muir; p. 35: Helene Dujardin; p. 61: vm2002/shutterstock; p. 71: Thomas J. Story; p. 92: © 2020 Nadine Greeff; p. 141: Bartosz Luczak/istock; p. 171: Oksana Bratanova/Alamy Stock Photo; p. 188: Elysa Weitala

Cover: Hand-Lettered Title: © 2020 Marco Marella

Author Photo: MacKenzie Morrison

Cover: Pad Thai Noodle Salad, page 85

ISBN: Print 978-1-64611-543-3 | eBook 978-1-64611-544-0

R0

FOR:

LOUISE

AND

T.E.D.

(Tonight's Exciting Dinner)

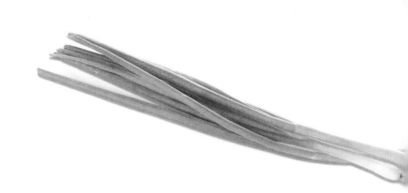

Contents

Introduction

WELCOME TO *THE COMPLETE COOKBOOK FOR TEENS*. I'm excited to be on this cooking adventure with you. Whether you've only been in the kitchen once or twice, are wanting to expand on your cooking techniques, or feel like you're ready to enter your favorite pie in the state fair, I have so many exciting tips and recipes to share with you.

We'll start with Get in the Kitchen, where we will get oriented and talk best cooking practices; it's a great place to begin. From there, you'll set up your workstation and the tools you'll need as you prepare for your cooking session, with helpful tips on how to read a recipe (and why you should reread it), what to wear, and why you should clean as you go.

We'll touch on cooking terminology, where you'll find a glossary for the terms and techniques you'll come across in this book to use as a reference for greater success. We'll also review kitchen safety, from knives to bacteria, and the proper precautions to keep in mind while working through a recipe.

Once we get these basics out of the way, you'll be ready to cook! Maybe the first recipe you'll try will be a breakfast dish, like Pumpkin Pancakes (page 18) or Asparagus Frittata (page 27). Maybe a snack is what you'll choose first, something for yourself like Chunky Guacamole (page 42) or perhaps Baked Chicken Wings (page 51) to share with friends and family.

You'll find plenty of recipes to prepare for yourself—delicious items like pizza, sandwiches, or homemade crepes. I'm also confident you have the skills to feed your entire family with a meatless meal like Vegetable Lasagna (page 97), or you can make meat the star attraction with Italian Roast Beef (page 132) or Chicken Enchiladas (page 133). There are even recipes for you to create a Thanksgiving-ready roasted turkey complete with gravy and fresh cranberry sauce (see pages 127, 128, and 129).

We'll wind down with sauces and dips, like homemade mayonnaise and barbecue sauces, and finish it all off with simple but impressive desserts such as Molten Caramel Cakes (page 167) and Peach and Berry Crisp (page 160).

I hope that as you make each recipe, your self-confidence in the kitchen grows and you try more challenging recipes that add more techniques and steps. Know that you won't always succeed. There will be recipe fails, and that's okay. The important thing is to learn from what happened and improve those skills for success next time.

Find a recipe that you love to cook and make it your signature dish. It doesn't have to be from this book, but there are plenty here to help you get started and develop your cooking skills as you set the foundation for your cooking journey.

Mostly, I hope you sit down with what you have cooked and take a moment to be proud of what you've created.

CHAPTER ONE

Get in the Kitchen

Welcome to the first chapter in your culinary quest. Before you begin cooking, set up your workstation so you have everything in one place. We'll also talk about the tools, terminology, and safety practices that will make you an efficient and successful chef in the kitchen.

Let's get started. You're one step closer to choosing, creating, and serving your first fantastic recipe.

Setting Up for Success

Setting up your workstation will ensure that you have all the ingredients for your recipe as well as the proper tools, attire, and safety measures needed to make your cooking experience successful.

* Read and reread the recipe.

* Figure out how much time you'll need, what ingredients to shop for, and any terms or techniques you'll need to look up first.

* Do a safety evaluation of your work area: Be sure your countertops and tools are clean, there aren't any fire hazards, and any pets are safely out of harm's way.

* Measure out all the ingredients and set them in recipe order: Chefs call this "mise en place," which is French for "everything in its place." You'll have a much easier time following a recipe if you don't need to scramble to find an ingredient while a saucepan is bubbling on the stove.

* Lay out the tools needed for the recipe: This includes any pots, pans, or utensils you'll need for a recipe as well as any special tools, like a blender or grater.

* Wear the proper attire: For safe cooking, you'll want to wear an apron, pull back your hair, and avoid loose-fitting sleeves that could catch on a burner or kitchen tool.

COOKING TERMINOLOGY

Cooking has its own language. This brief glossary can be a reference for techniques you come across in this book that may be unfamiliar to you.

Al dente: refers to pasta that is still firm to the bite, not soft or overcooked

Broil: to cook food in an oven directly under the heat source

Caramelize: to break down sugars in vegetables or fruit by cooking slowly to create a golden-brown color

Deglaze: to add a liquid such as broth to a hot pan after cooking meat to pick up the concentrated flavors and sediments left in the pan

Drippings: the liquid that remains after roasting meat, often used to make gravy

Julienne: to slice foods into skinny strips (1/16- to 1/8-inch thick)

Pare: to remove the thin outer layer of fruits or vegetables with a small knife or peeler

Prep: to prepare ingredients or equipment as the recipe directs (e.g., greasing a pan, peeling potatoes)

Roux: a thickener made of equal parts fat and flour that is slowly cooked

Whip: to beat ingredients by hand or with an electric mixer to add air into the ingredients until they are light and fluffy (like butter and sugar)

Whisk: to blend or incorporate ingredients with a quick, light brushing motion

Zest: to remove the rind of citrus using an angle-bladed tool called a zester

Safety First!

Safety is essential in the kitchen, regardless of your skill level. Being mindful of safety can prevent disaster and keep the fun in cooking without incident.

BLADES

Choosing the right knife: For these recipes, you'll want an all-purpose knife that can chop, mince, and slice.

How to hold the knife: Wrap your fingers around the knife's handle for a firm grip. Keep your hand behind the bolster, where the handle meets the blade. Keep the sharp part of the knife, the edge, down.

Make sure the knife is sharp: A sharp knife cuts easily and safely. A dull blade rips and tears because it requires more pressure to do the job.

How to wash a knife: Never drop a knife into a sink of dishwater, where someone may accidentally grab the sharp end beneath the foam. Instead, wash it immediately with warm, soapy water, and put it away.

BURNS

Use oven mitts: Protect your hands and wrists with long oven mitts while inserting items into or removing items from a hot oven.

Check your oven before cooking: Open the oven door, remove any pots or pans, and adjust the racks before turning it on to preheat.

Avoid loose clothing: Wearing an apron will keep your clothing tight. Secure all loose clothing.

Treat burns quickly: If you've burned yourself, immediately place the burn under cool running water. Avoid butter, oil, and creams, which can worsen a burn and prevent healing.

Know how to put out a grease fire: This is the most common type of fire in the kitchen. Never use water to put out a grease fire (it will make it worse). Instead, use a lid to smother small pan fires or a fire extinguisher for bigger fires.

MICROWAVE HACKS

The microwave is a great kitchen appliance. Most people only use it to reheat food, but it is capable of so much more.

Soak beans: Add three cups of water per cup of beans and microwave them for 15 minutes. Let the beans rest for one hour.

Roast nuts: Place the nuts in a single layer on a plate and microwave them for one minute. Repeat until the nuts are roasted to your liking.

Peel fruits and vegetables: Peaches or tomatoes work best for this hack, which makes peeling produce easier. Cut the fruit in half, place it on a plate, and microwave it until the skin wrinkles. Peel the microwaved fruit with a fork.

Freshen a stale loaf of bread: Wrap the bread in a damp paper towel and microwave it for eight minutes on high.

BACTERIA

Don't ruin your efforts in the kitchen by introducing bacteria to your food or surfaces.

Put it away: Put away temperature-sensitive foods immediately, especially dairy products, raw meat, poultry, and seafood.

Wash your hands often: Be sure to use soap and warm water to prevent the spread of bacteria.

Use separate cutting boards: Keep your cutting board for raw meat separate from the one you use for vegetables and fruit.

Rinse fruits and vegetables: Soak fresh fruits and vegetables in a mixture of one cup white vinegar to four cups water for 20 minutes to remove bacteria and reduce pesticides.

Wipe down surfaces: Use warm, soapy water to wipe down surfaces before and after cooking.

10 ways to Be a Better Cook

Like all things worth learning, cooking takes practice. This is true no matter how much experience you have or how old you are.

When my grandmother was in her seventies, she once went to visit her sisters. She came home excited because they taught her how to make her bread better. She had been making the same bread recipe since she was a little girl, and her sisters had, too. They shared their best practices, and Grandma learned she was kneading too much flour into her dough.

Here are my top 10 ways to be a better cook:

1. **Learn from your mistakes:** You are going to have recipes fail. It's okay. It's a learning opportunity or sometimes just a bad day.

   At my house, my children call this my "company cooking" because I can make the same recipe 100 times, but when a guest comes for dinner, that same recipe is a disaster.

   Of course, it's disappointing when a recipe doesn't come together as you wanted. Don't be discouraged and don't give up. Enjoy the journey and keep cooking.

2. **Read and reread the recipe:** Read through the recipe to get a feel for the process and what you need. Reread the recipe to see if you need to look up any cooking terminology and evaluate if you have the proper ingredients. I read through the recipe again each time I add a new ingredient to make certain I'm adding the correct measurement and not overlooking a technique or ingredient. This is so important I'm saying it twice!

3. **Follow the recipe:** I always follow a new recipe precisely the first time I make it. Then, I listen to what those eating it have to say and make a note so that the next time I make the recipe, I can make adjustments to better fit the taste palates of those I'm feeding.

   For example, some people don't like the taste of cilantro. If you're making salsa and you know this, try substituting fresh basil, oregano, or parsley, or even a combination of these.

4. **Ask for help:** Even as an adult, I still call my mom to ask cooking questions. She has been cooking longer than me and has a lot of information to offer. Asking someone about a recipe can also help you understand why you're doing something, like combining the dry ingredients separately from the wet ingredients (because they mix more evenly) or bringing something to a temperature (to reduce, solidify, or change the structure).

5. **Use quality ingredients:** The quality of your ingredients plays a significant role in the outcome of your dish. Always use the best ingredients you can, and use fresh ingredients whenever possible. But don't mistake expensive ingredients for quality ones. You can visit a farmer's market for quality produce or a local butcher for great cuts of meat that fit your budget.

6. **Season to taste:** Follow the recipe as it is written, and then taste as you go, adding seasoning to your liking. You want the flavors to combine so that no seasoning overpowers the others.

7. **Clean as you go:** Take a few moments to clean your workstation as you work through the recipe. Dispose of vegetable peels when you finish, put away ingredients as you use them, and clean up spills as they happen. If there are a few minutes when the food is simmering or cooking, maximize this time by washing dishes. You'll be able to spend more time enjoying the meal you've made and less time dealing with a big mess afterward.

8. **Plate like a chef:** You worked hard to create something delicious, so be sure to show it off with plating. You can think of the plate as the face of a clock and place your protein, starch, and vegetables in the positions of a clock's two, six, and 10. Also, using odd numbers (e.g., three or five shrimp on a plate, not two or four) gives the impression of more food, and you can always add color with an edible garnish, such as parsley sprigs, sprinkles of fresh herbs, or slices of fresh fruit.

9. **Try new things:** Be open to new food experiences. Take a bite of something you've never tried. See if you can identify spices or ingredients by taste. Look at a dish's texture. Is it dense or fluffy? Is the sauce thick or thin? What else do you see, smell, and taste? By trying new things, you might learn about a new spice or herb and what food it would complement. If you don't like something the first time you taste it, try it cooked differently.

10. **Perfect your signature dish:** Find something you love to cook and make it your signature dish. Practice making it, ask for feedback, and be proud of the final dish.

RECIPE REALITY

Cooking can be flexible, and a good cook knows how to adjust and adapt in the kitchen. The more you cook, the more you'll be able to use a recipe as a guideline for your own tastes. Everyone has a different palate. Some people like more spice in their food, and some might prefer a milder dish.

If a recipe doesn't turn out right, view it as a learning opportunity and try again, keeping note of the changes you can work in to make it a success. If a recipe seems like it's missing something, you can add an ingredient that might make it more appealing to your palate. In many of my recipes, I've included suggestions for experimenting with different ingredients you can swap in. As you learn more about what you like and how to build flavor in a dish, feel free to adjust the recipes in this book to appeal to your taste.

About the Recipes

The recipes in this book were chosen to give you a variety of options. You'll find plenty of classics, like pancakes, roasts, and pizza, as well as new spins on traditional dishes.

There's a Classic Lemonade (page 38) recipe with a variation to show you how you can use a basic recipe as a foundation for another beverage. There are roasts, soups, and casseroles. You'll even learn how to make your own sauces like mayonnaise, hollandaise, and steak sauce.

Each chapter features a collection of simple recipes in the beginning, followed by some recipes that are more technical so the chapter can grow with you as your cooking skills develop. You'll find it easy to recognize the difficulty of the recipes with my rating system:

▲△△   One triangle indicates the recipe is easy to execute with basic cooking skills and fewer ingredients and involves little to no cooking.

▲▲△   Two triangles are used for recipes that may require a skill you might not have much experience with or involve different cooking methods.

▲▲▲   Three triangles are for recipes that include one or more skills you may not know, more than one cooking method, or a lengthier prep or cooking time. These recipes are more complex but create something a little more special.

Many recipes have tips that will help you develop additional skills or give a more in-depth definition of a new technique. Also, for the recipes with a Gluten-Free label, please remember to always check ingredient packaging for gluten-free labeling to ensure that all foods, especially oats, were processed in a completely gluten-free facility.

Cantaloupe Bowls, page 12

CHAPTER TWO

Breakfast

Cantaloupe Bowls

▲△△

EXTRA QUICK   GLUTEN-FREE   VEGETARIAN

PREP TIME: 5 minutes / **TOTAL TIME:** 5 minutes
MAKES: 2 bowls

Nature provides the bowl for this refreshing breakfast or snack packed with any type of berries you like. Feel free to use raspberries, blackberries, blueberries, strawberries, or a combination of them all. The Maple Granola (page 15) is excellent here, or you can stick with store-bought granola if you're short on time. You can also experiment with different yogurts or cottage cheese.

1 large cantaloupe
1 cup plain Greek yogurt
½ cup fresh berries
1 cup granola

1. Slice the cantaloupe in half along the widest point. Cut about ½ inch off the bottom of each cantaloupe half so that each bowl rests flat on a plate. Scoop out the seeds with a spoon.

2. Add ½ cup of the yogurt to the center of each cantaloupe half. Top with fresh berries and granola.

> **JAZZ IT UP:** There are so many delicious ways to dress up your cantaloupe. Try using fresh mint, nuts, sliced grapes, and more.

Impossible Quiche

▲△△

EXTRA QUICK   NUT-FREE   VEGETARIAN

PREP TIME: 10 minutes / **COOK TIME:** 11 minutes / **TOTAL TIME:** 21 minutes
MAKES: 6 servings

You might have thought quiche was a tricky technical dish until now. This quiche whips up fast and is cooked in the microwave! My friend, Sherri, shared this with me, and I was amazed at how easily it all comes together. It's an impressive breakfast that you'll turn to when you want something a little more substantial without too much time to prepare it. Try garnishing it with chopped green onions, sour cream, or salsa.

FOR THE CRUST

½ cup vegetable oil

2 tablespoons milk

1½ cups flour

1 teaspoon salt

2 tablespoons soy sauce

FOR THE FILLING

3 eggs

½ cup half-and-half

½ teaspoon hot sauce

1 cup grated
mozzarella cheese

1 (6-ounce) can French
fried onion rings

TO MAKE THE CRUST

1. In an 8-inch microwave safe pie dish, combine the oil, milk, flour, and salt. Working with your hands, mix the ingredients until you have a dough you can press into the pan to form the pie crust. Brush the crust with the soy sauce.

TO MAKE THE FILLING

2. In a medium mixing bowl, combine the eggs, half-and-half, and hot sauce. Beat the mixture until well combined.

3. Add the cheese to the top of the pie crust. Pour the egg mixture over the cheese. Sprinkle with the onion rings. Set the microwave to 50 percent power and cook the quiche for 11 minutes, until it is set.

> **PRO TIP:** Be sure to press the crust firmly into the pie dish so that it evenly covers the bottom and sides of the entire dish with no holes or cracks. This will keep the filling from leaking out and ensure that you have picture-perfect slices when you serve it.
>
> **JAZZ IT UP:** Try adding crumbled bacon to the dish.

Gluten-Free French Toast Casserole

▲△△

GLUTEN-FREE   NUT-FREE   VEGETARIAN

PREP TIME: 24 hours / **COOK TIME:** 45 minutes / **TOTAL TIME:** 24 hours 45 minutes
SERVES: 6

This recipe starts the night before, giving the bread time to soak up the custard and creating an incredibly rich French toast dish. This is one of my go-to recipes, whether I have company or I just want a special but easy breakfast. Using a blender creates a silky smooth custard, but you can also whisk the eggs by hand until fluffy if you don't have a blender in your kitchen.

4 ounces cream cheese

4 large eggs

¾ cup milk

⅔ cup half-and-half

¼ cup maple syrup

1 teaspoon vanilla extract

½ teaspoon salt

1 (15-ounce) loaf gluten-free cinnamon raisin bread, cubed

1. Blend the cream cheese, eggs, milk, half-and-half, maple syrup, vanilla, and salt in a blender until fully combined and smooth.

2. Grease an 8-by-8-inch baking pan. Place the bread in an even layer in the pan, then pour the egg mixture over the bread. Press the bread down to soak up the egg mixture. Cover the pan with aluminum foil and refrigerate overnight.

3. In the morning, preheat the oven to 350°F. Remove the aluminum foil and place the pan in the oven on the center rack. Bake for 45 minutes, or until golden brown.

SUB IN: This dish also works excellently with any stale bread or bagels you need to use up. Just be sure to double check your bread's label if your guests follow a gluten-free diet.

JAZZ IT UP: Dust this dish with powdered sugar and add fresh berries as a topping.

Maple Granola

▲ △ △

DAIRY-FREE   VEGAN

PREP TIME: 10 minutes / **COOK TIME:** 1 hour 15 minutes /
TOTAL TIME: 1 hour 25 minutes
MAKES: about 6 cups

Baking this granola will make your entire home smell amazing. When it's done, it makes a great snack on its own or a crunchy topping for yogurt, or you can pour it into a bowl and add some milk for homemade granola cereal. I love the textures and flavors, and it's incredibly filling!

Nonstick cooking spray

3 cups oats (not instant oats)

1 cup slivered almonds

1 cup cashews

1 cup shredded sweetened coconut

½ cup light brown sugar

½ cup maple syrup

¼ cup extra-virgin olive oil

1 teaspoon salt

1 cup dried cranberries or raisins

1½ cups maple-glazed walnuts

1. Preheat the oven to 250°F. Line two 13-by-9-inch pans with aluminum foil or parchment paper and spray them with nonstick cooking spray. Combine the oats, almonds, cashews, coconut, and brown sugar in a large mixing bowl.

2. In a separate bowl, combine the maple syrup, olive oil, and salt, and stir. Pour the wet mixture into the bowl with the oats mixture and toss to coat. Spread the mixture evenly onto the prepared baking pans.

3. Place the pans in the preheated oven and bake for 1 hour and 15 minutes, stirring every 15 minutes to give the granola an even color.

4. Remove the granola from the oven and transfer it into a large bowl. Add the cranberries and maple-glazed walnuts and mix until evenly distributed. Store it in an airtight container for up to 4 weeks.

JAZZ IT UP: You can use any nuts, seeds, or dried fruit you like in this granola, or even add in chocolate chips at the end. Just be sure to let the granola cool before adding any ingredients that might melt.

Basic Omelet

▲△△

EXTRA QUICK   GLUTEN-FREE   NUT-FREE   VEGETARIAN

PREP TIME: 5 minutes / **COOK TIME:** 10 minutes / **TOTAL TIME:** 15 minutes
SERVES: 4

Omelets require a little more work than scrambled eggs. However, they're well worth the effort since you can create endless omelet varieties to please anyone from meat lovers to vegetarians. See the variations at the end of this recipe for some ideas.

6 eggs

⅓ cup milk

1 teaspoon salt

⅛ teaspoon freshly ground black pepper

1½ tablespoons butter

1. In a large mixing bowl, beat the eggs using an electric hand mixer on high, or by hand, just to blend the yolks and the whites. Add the milk, salt, and pepper and beat thoroughly.

2. In a medium skillet over medium-high heat, melt the butter, and then tip the skillet to spread butter to the sides and bottom of the pan. Reduce the heat to low, pour the egg mixture into the skillet, and cook until a film of cooked egg has formed on the bottom of the pan. Lift the edge of the cooked egg with a spatula and tilt the pan so that the uncooked portion runs under the raised, cooked portion. Continue cooking until a film of cooked egg forms, then repeat the lifting and cooking process for about 10 minutes, until the entire mixture is cooked and golden brown on the bottom. Loosen the omelet from the pan with a spatula, fold it from the handle of the skillet to the opposite side of the pan, and turn it onto a plate.

PRO TIP: The lower the heat and the slower you cook your omelet, the better the texture will be.

Omelet Variations:

BACON OMELET:

Crumble six slices of crispy bacon over the surface of the omelet while cooking.

CHEESE OMELET:

Add ⅓ cup of grated cheddar cheese over the omelet as it cooks.

MUSHROOM OMELET:

Scatter one cup of sautéed sliced mushrooms on the omelet as it cooks.

SPANISH OMELET:

Add three tablespoons of chunky salsa to the egg mixture before pouring it into the pan.

MEAT OMELET:

Add ⅓ cup of heated, diced, and cooked meat (e.g., chicken, ham, or steak) to the omelet just before folding it.

VEGETABLE OMELET:

In a small skillet, add two tablespoons of minced onion and two tablespoons of butter and cook for about seven minutes, until tender. Add one cup of peas, diced celery, or asparagus tips and heat it until warm. Add the vegetable mixture to the omelet just before folding.

Pumpkin Pancakes

▲△△

EXTRA QUICK   NUT-FREE   VEGETARIAN

PREP TIME: 5 minutes / **COOK TIME:** 10 minutes / **TOTAL TIME:** 15 minutes
SERVES: 4

Pancakes are a classic breakfast, and these delicious pumpkin pancakes are filled with warm goodness that's perfect for enjoying on a crisp fall day. They have protein to keep you full and a delicious pumpkin flavor that pairs well with butter and maple syrup. Try serving them with warm applesauce.

1 cup cottage cheese

1 cup pumpkin puree

3 tablespoons flour

2 eggs

4 tablespoons vegetable oil

½ teaspoon ground cardamom

4 tablespoons butter, divided

1. In a blender or food processor, combine the cottage cheese, pumpkin puree, flour, and eggs until smooth. Add the oil and cardamom, then pulse to blend.

2. In a pan over medium-high heat, melt 1 tablespoon of the butter. Add ⅓ cup batter to the pan, pouring in a "puddle" to make the pancake. Cook for 2 to 3 minutes, or until batter begins to bubble. Using a spatula, gently turn the pancake over and cook the other side for 2 to 3 minutes. Repeat this process until the batter is gone.

PRO TIP: To cook more than one pancake at a time, just allow space between the batter as you pour it in the pan. If the pancakes run into each other, you can separate them by pressing with the edge of the spatula to cut the pancakes away from one another.

Microwave Egg Casserole

▲△△

EXTRA QUICK   NUT-FREE

PREP TIME: 5 minutes / **COOK TIME:** 15 minutes / **TOTAL TIME:** 20 minutes
SERVES: 2

Food brings people together. My friend, Sherri, and I love to talk all things food, and she shared this Microwave Egg Casserole with me, which was her mother's recipe. It couldn't be easier, and it takes less than 30 minutes from start to finish. It's a great, hearty breakfast with plenty of savory flavor, and I think you'll enjoy it.

6 slices bacon

1½ tablespoons butter

¼ cup chopped
green pepper

4 eggs

½ cup cream of
mushroom soup

1. Place the bacon on a microwavable plate and cover it with a paper towel. Place it in the microwave and cook on high for 7 minutes.

2. In a small microwavable dish, add the butter and green pepper. Cook in the microwave on high for 1 minute.

3. Beat the eggs and the soup together. Add the butter and green pepper to the egg mixture and stir to combine. Pour the mixture into a microwavable dish and cook on medium-high for 5 minutes, stirring often. Let it rest for 1 minute, and then sprinkle it with bacon.

SUB IN: Skip the bacon or use a bacon substitute to make this recipe vegetarian. Just be sure to follow the cooking instructions on the package if you're using a vegetarian bacon substitute.

JAZZ IT UP: Add one tablespoon of salsa to the soup and egg mixture before cooking.

Pineapple Coconut Pancakes

▲△△

EXTRA QUICK NUT-FREE VEGETARIAN

PREP TIME: 10 minutes / **COOK TIME:** 15 minutes / **TOTAL TIME:** 25 minutes
MAKES: 6 to 8 (4-ounce) pancakes

These light and fluffy pancakes bring the flavors of the tropics with plenty of pineapple topped with sweetened coconut flakes. Drizzling maple syrup over a stack of these is particularly delicious, though you can reinvent them with a variety of other toppings.

1 cup pancake mix

¼ cup coconut milk

¼ cup canned pineapple chunks, ½ cup syrup reserved

4 tablespoons butter, divided

⅓ cup maple syrup

Sweetened coconut flakes, for garnish

1. In a medium mixing bowl, combine the pancake mix, coconut milk, and reserved pineapple syrup. Stir until well mixed.

2. Melt 1 tablespoon of the butter in a pan over medium-low heat. For each pancake, pour ⅓ cup of the batter into the hot pan, pouring it into a "puddle." Press 6 to 8 pineapple chunks into the batter and let the pancake cook for about 1 minute, or until it begins to bubble. Using a spatula, carefully flip the pancake, so the pineapple chunks stay intact. Cook for 1 minute on this side. If you are up for the challenge, you can cook more than one pancake in the pan—just keep some space between each pancake. Repeat this process until the batter is gone.

3. Plate the pancakes and serve them with warm maple syrup drizzled over the top and garnished with toasted coconut and additional pineapple, if you like.

JAZZ IT UP: Instead of garnishing with maple syrup and coconut flakes, try topping the pancakes with whipped cream and sprinkling them with cinnamon.

Raisin Bran Muffins

▲△△

PREP TIME: 15 minutes / **COOK TIME:** 10 minutes / **TOTAL TIME:** 25 minutes
MAKES: 18 muffins

··

These muffins are easy to make and turn old-fashioned raisin bran cereal into a fresh, irresistible treat. They also store well in the refrigerator or freezer, giving you breakfast on the go in seconds.

1¼ cups all-purpose flour

½ cup sugar

1¼ teaspoons baking soda

½ teaspoon salt

1⅔ cups raisin and
   bran cereal

1 cup milk

¼ cup vegetable oil

1 egg, beaten

1. Preheat the oven to 400°F. Grease a muffin tin or use cupcake liners. In a large mixing bowl, combine the flour, sugar, baking soda, and salt. Stir in the cereal.

2. In a medium bowl, combine the milk, oil, and beaten egg. Mix well by hand. Add the wet mixture to the dry ingredients and stir by hand until well combined.

3. Add 3 tablespoons of batter to each muffin cup (or fill ⅔ full, depending on the size of the cups) and bake for 15 minutes. The muffins are done when a knife inserted in the center of one comes out clean. Store the muffins in an airtight container in the refrigerator, or freeze them for up to 2 months.

HELPFUL HINT: If you have leftovers, pop one in the microwave for 10 seconds for a warm muffin.

JAZZ IT UP: Sprinkle the top of your muffins with coarse sugar before baking them for an extra sweet crunch.

Baked Egg Casserole

△△△

NUT-FREE

PREP TIME: 15 minutes / **COOK TIME:** 45 minutes / **TOTAL TIME:** 1 hour
SERVES: 6 to 8

This egg casserole is stuffed with all your favorite breakfast foods. It's perfect for a substantial meal in the morning for breakfast or for dinner in the evening. You can even prepare it the night before and simply pop it in the oven about an hour before you're ready to serve it.

8 ounces
mushrooms, sliced

1 pound bulk
sausage, crumbled

6 large eggs, beaten

2 cups milk

1 pound cheddar
cheese, cubed

1 teaspoon salt

1 teaspoon dry mustard

2 slices white bread, cubed

1. Preheat the oven to 350°F. Grease an 8-by-12-inch pan.

2. In a large skillet over medium heat, cook the mushrooms and sausage for about 8 minutes, until the sausage is browned and the mushrooms begin to wilt. Drain the grease and set the cooked sausage and mushrooms aside.

3. In a large mixing bowl, combine the eggs, milk, cheese, salt, and mustard. Mix well to combine.

4. Add the cubed bread to the prepared pan. Add the sausage and mushrooms to the egg mixture, then pour it into the prepared pan and cover it with aluminum foil.

5. Place the covered pan on the center rack in the preheated oven and bake for 45 minutes until set (a knife inserted in the center should come out clean). Let it stand for 5 to 10 minutes before serving.

> **PRO TIP:** This dish is even better if you let the uncooked casserole sit in the refrigerator overnight, and then bake it the next day.
>
> **SUB IN:** Use one pound of crumbled cooked bacon in place of the sausage.

Buckwheat Cakes

▲△△

EXTRA QUICK   NUT-FREE   VEGETARIAN

PREP TIME: 10 minutes / **COOK TIME:** 20 minutes / **TOTAL TIME:** 30 minutes
SERVES: 4

. . . .

These pancakes are made with buckwheat flour for a pancake that's both fluffy and filling. I like to serve these buckwheat cakes hot and top them with berries, sliced peaches or nectarines, apple butter, or classic maple syrup.

½ cup sifted bread flour

2 teaspoons sugar

1 teaspoon baking soda

½ teaspoon baking powder

½ teaspoon salt

1½ cups buckwheat flour

3¼ cups buttermilk

2 tablespoons vegetable oil

4 teaspoons butter, divided

1. In a large mixing bowl, combine the bread flour, sugar, baking soda, baking powder, and salt. Add the buckwheat flour and mix well.

2. In a separate, large mixing bowl, pour in the buttermilk and oil and mix together. Add the dry ingredients and beat them together only until the mixture is well blended.

3. Heat 1 teaspoon of the butter in a large skillet over medium-low heat for 30 seconds. Add ⅓ cup of the batter and cook for about 2 minutes, until bubbles appear on the surface of the batter. Using a spatula, gently flip the pancake over and cook for about 2 minutes, until golden brown. Repeat this process until the batter is gone.

SUB IN: If you don't have buttermilk on hand, try adding one tablespoon of white distilled vinegar to plain milk and letting it rest for five minutes.

JAZZ IT UP: Add two tablespoons of sesame seeds to the batter before cooking it in the skillet.

zucchini omelet

▲▲△

PREP TIME: 10 minutes / **COOK TIME:** 20 minutes / **TOTAL TIME:** 30 minutes
SERVES: 4

....

This omelet is stuffed with a great combination of flavorful vegetables. If you've already made my Basic Omelet (page 16), this twist on the classic will be a breeze to cook up. Top it with cheese before serving if you like.

3 tablespoons extra-virgin olive oil

3 small green onions, finely minced

1 garlic clove, finely minced

5 small zucchinis, thinly sliced

1 large fresh tomato, peeled and diced

½ teaspoon salt

¼ teaspoon freshly ground black pepper

1 teaspoon dried parsley

9 eggs

1. Heat the oil in a medium skillet over medium-high heat for 30 seconds. Add the onion and sauté for about 7 minutes, until tender. Add the garlic and stir for about 30 seconds, just until fragrant. Add the zucchini, tomato, salt, pepper, and parsley. Reduce the heat to medium-low and cook for 5 minutes, or until the zucchini is tender. Remove from heat.

2. In a large mixing bowl, lightly beat the eggs. Add the vegetables and stir until coated. Pour the mixture back into the skillet. Tightly cover the pan and cook over low heat for about 8 minutes, until the edges of the omelet pull away from the pan, or until the egg is mostly firm. If the center puffs up, prick it with a sharp knife.

3. Remove the lid. When the omelet is firm, put it on a plate, slice it like a pie, and serve.

JAZZ IT UP: Try topping the omelet with sour cream or salsa.

Cheesy Cauliflower Bake

▲ ▲ △

GLUTEN-FREE   NUT-FREE   VEGETARIAN

PREP TIME: 10 minutes / **COOK TIME:** 50 minutes / **TOTAL TIME:** 1 hour
SERVES: 4

This recipe is a great substitute for a hash brown dish, and cauliflower replaces potatoes without missing out on texture or flavor. It all comes together with a creamy, cheesy sauce. Add more cayenne pepper if you prefer a little more heat.

Nonstick cooking spray

1 tablespoon butter

1 large onion, diced

2 garlic cloves, minced

5 cups shredded cauliflower

1 cup shredded cheddar cheese

¼ cup green bell pepper, seeded and finely chopped

⅓ cup sour cream

2 tablespoons light cream cheese, softened

½ teaspoon salt

¼ teaspoon freshly ground black pepper

¼ teaspoon cayenne pepper

¼ cup Parmesan cheese

1. Preheat the oven to 350°F. Prepare a 9-by-9-inch baking dish with nonstick cooking spray.

2. Melt the butter in a medium skillet over medium heat. Add the onion and cook for about 8 minutes, until soft and starting to brown. Stir in the garlic and cook just until fragrant.

3. In a large bowl, combine the cooked onion and garlic mixture with the cauliflower, cheddar cheese, bell pepper, sour cream, cream cheese, salt, black pepper, and cayenne pepper. Stir until well combined. Spread it evenly in the prepared baking dish. The mixture will seem dry but will become moister as the cauliflower cooks.

4. Bake for 30 minutes, then remove it from the oven. Stir the casserole and evenly spread it out to the corners of the pan. Sprinkle the Parmesan cheese on top and return it to the oven. Bake for another 15 to 20 minutes, until the cauliflower is soft and the cheese is melty. Serve hot.

JAZZ IT UP: Use red, yellow, and/or orange bell peppers in place of the green for added color.

Savory Cheese Biscuits

▲▲△

NUT-FREE   VEGETARIAN

PREP TIME: 20 minutes / **COOK TIME:** 12 minutes / **TOTAL TIME:** 35 minutes
MAKES: about 12 biscuits

With the addition of cheddar cheese and cayenne pepper, basic biscuits become a savory delight with a bit of a kick. You can serve these biscuits as a side to your favorite dish, top them with gravy, or slice one open and add a sausage patty or egg.

Butter, for greasing

2 cups all-purpose flour, plus extra for dusting

2 teaspoons double-acting baking powder

1 teaspoon salt

5 tablespoons cold butter

¾ cup milk

1 cup grated cheddar cheese

1 teaspoon cayenne pepper

1. Preheat the oven to 450°F. Butter a baking sheet.

2. In a large bowl, combine the flour, baking powder, and salt. Using a pastry blender or two knives, cut the cold butter into the flour mixture until the butter pieces are the size of peas. Stir in the milk gradually to create a soft dough. Add the cheddar cheese and cayenne pepper and combine well.

3. Knead dough on a lightly floured cutting board for 30 seconds. Roll out the dough with a rolling pin until it is ½ inch thick. Press a biscuit cutter in a bit of flour and cut the rolled dough into circles. Place the biscuit rounds on the prepared baking sheet.

4. Bake the biscuits on the center rack in the pre-heated oven for 12 minutes, or until the biscuits are golden brown.

> **JAZZ IT UP:** Try different blends of cheese in these biscuits. I recommend three-quarters of a cup of cheddar and a quarter cup of Parmesan, or half a cup of cheddar and half a cup of Colby Jack.

Asparagus Frittata

▲▲△

GLUTEN-FREE   NUT-FREE   VEGETARIAN

PREP TIME: 15 minutes / **COOK TIME:** 35 minutes / **TOTAL TIME:** 50 minutes
SERVES: 4

This frittata is a delicious egg dish filled with asparagus and topped with cheese. Instead of milk, I use cottage cheese for a richer, creamier frittata. Feel free to use the base of the recipe (five eggs, ¾ cup of cottage cheese, two cups of vegetables or meat) and experiment with different add-ins to create your own spin on this recipe.

1 (10-ounce) package
   frozen cut asparagus, or
   ½ pound fresh asparagus

5 large eggs

¾ cup low-fat
   cottage cheese

2 teaspoons mustard

½ teaspoon salt

⅛ teaspoon freshly ground
   black pepper

3 tablespoons extra-virgin
   olive oil

1 cup sliced
   fresh mushrooms

1 small onion, diced

¼ cup grated
   cheddar cheese

1 small tomato, cut into
   wedges, or ¼ cup
   chopped tomato

1. Preheat the oven to 400°F.

2. Cook the frozen asparagus according to the package directions. Drain and set aside. If using fresh asparagus, cut off and discard the tough bottoms of the stalks (about 1-½ inches) and place the green parts of the stalks in a wide pan with enough water to cover them. Bring the water to a boil and cook for 8 to 10 minutes, or until crisp-tender, then drain. Reserve two spears for garnish; cut the remaining asparagus into one-inch pieces.

3. While the asparagus cooks, beat the eggs in a medium mixing bowl until foamy. Add the cottage cheese, mustard, salt, and pepper and beat with an electric mixer or by hand. Set aside.

CONTINUED >

. . . .

4. Heat the olive oil in a large, ovenproof skillet over medium heat. Add the mushrooms and onion and cook for about 7 minutes, until just tender (the mushrooms will begin to wilt and the onion will become translucent). Stir in the asparagus pieces. Pour the egg mixture over the mushrooms and asparagus. Reduce the heat to low and allow the mixture to cook for 5 minutes, or until it begins to bubble slightly and set around the edges of the skillet.

5. Place the frittata in the preheated oven and bake for 10 minutes, or until it is set and a knife inserted in center comes out clean. Top the frittata with the cheese as soon as you pull it out of the oven. Garnish each serving with the tomato.

PRO TIP: Let the frittata rest in the skillet for five minutes before slicing it.

Blueberry Zucchini Bread

▲▲△

DAIRY-FREE | NUT-FREE | VEGETARIAN

PREP TIME: 15 minutes / **COOK TIME:** 50 minutes / **TOTAL TIME:** 1 hour 5 minutes
MAKES: 1 (9-by-5-inch) loaf

This is the perfect zucchini bread with the addition of plump, juicy blueberries. Plus, it's a batter bread, so there's no waiting for yeast to rise. Just mix, pour, bake, and enjoy. For an extra treat, try toasting the bread and spreading it with butter.

1 cup plus 2 tablespoons sugar *(used all at once)*

½ cup vegetable oil

2 medium eggs, beaten

1½ teaspoons vanilla extract

1 cup shredded zucchini

1½ cups all-purpose flour

1½ teaspoons ground cinnamon

½ teaspoon salt

½ teaspoon baking powder

⅛ teaspoon baking soda

1 cup fresh blueberries

1. Preheat the oven to 350°F. Lightly grease a 9-by-5-inch loaf pan.

2. In a large bowl, add the sugar, oil, eggs, and vanilla and beat by hand or with an electric hand mixer until well combined. Fold in the zucchini, and then mix in the flour, cinnamon, salt, baking powder, and baking soda. Gently fold in the blueberries. Transfer the batter to the prepared loaf pan.

3. Place the pan on the center rack in the preheated oven and bake for 50 minutes, or until a knife inserted in the center of the loaf comes out clean. Let cool in the pan for 20 minutes. Using oven mitts, turn the loaf out of the pan and onto wire racks to cool completely.

JAZZ IT UP: You can fold half a cup of chopped walnuts into the batter before transferring it to the pan.

Sausage Breakfast Casserole

▲ ▲ △

NUT-FREE

PREP TIME: 15 minutes, plus 8 hours refrigeration /
COOK TIME: 45 minutes / **TOTAL TIME:** 9 hours
SERVES: 8 to 10

You'll need to let this casserole sit overnight, but it's quick to throw together and worth the wait. In the morning, just wake up, put it in the oven, and sit down to a delicious hot breakfast. You can also prepare it in the morning and bake it for dinner.

10 premade
   homestyle biscuits

2 tablespoons
   butter, softened

1 pound bulk pork sausage

1 cup chopped onion

1½ cups shredded
   cheddar cheese

8 eggs

2 cups milk

1 teaspoon salt

1. Grease a 13-by-9-by-2-inch baking dish. Spread the biscuits with the butter and place them in the prepared pan.

2. In a medium skillet, cook the sausage with the onion for about 8 minutes, until the sausage is brown and the onion is translucent. Drain well and break the sausage up into small pieces. Spoon the sausage and onion mixture over the biscuits and sprinkle them with cheese.

3. In a large mixing bowl, combine the eggs, milk, and salt. Mix well by hand or with an electric mixer, and then pour the mixture over the biscuits. Cover the casserole with aluminum foil and place it in the refrigerator overnight.

4. When ready to bake, preheat the oven to 350°F. Remove the casserole from the refrigerator 15 minutes before baking. Bake uncovered on the center rack for 45 minutes, or until set.

JAZZ IT UP: Add some spice to this dish with one (4-ounce) can of whole green chilis, drained and seeded. While the sausage is cooking, add the green chilis to the bottom of the baking dish. You may need to use kitchen scissors to open each chili so it rests flat on the bottom of the pan.

Preserves and Cream Biscuits

▲▲△

EXTRA QUICK   NUT-FREE   VEGETARIAN

PREP TIME: 15 minutes / **COOKING TIME:** 15 minutes / **TOTAL TIME:** 30 minutes
SERVES: 6

These sweet biscuits are fun to make and a treat to eat. I love them fresh out of the oven, but they're also delicious the next day. Try these with any type of preserves you like.

1 cup heavy (whipping) cream

3 cups pancake and baking mix (such as Bisquick)

¼ cup preserves

2 tablespoons cream cheese, softened

2 teaspoons sugar

1. Preheat the oven to 400°F. Very lightly grease a cookie sheet or 13-by-9-by-2-inch baking dish.

2. In a large bowl, combine the cream with the baking mix just until moistened; it will be more dry than wet. Lightly flour a flat surface, such as a cutting board, and turn the dough onto it. Knead the dough about 10 times by pushing the dough away from you with the heel of your hand, and then reshaping it into a ball and repeating.

3. Using a rolling pin, roll the dough into a ½-inch thick rectangle. Use a 2-inch round cutter and cut out the biscuits. Place the cut biscuits onto the prepared pan. Press the rounded side of a teaspoon into the top of each biscuit, making an indentation in the center.

4. In a small bowl, combine the preserves and cream cheese and mix by hand or with an electric mixer until smooth and well combined. Drop a teaspoon of filling into the indentation on each biscuit. Sprinkle the tops with sugar.

5. Place the prepared biscuits on the center oven rack and bake for 12 to 15 minutes, or until golden brown. They are best served warm. Do NOT freeze them. Leftover biscuits can be placed in an airtight container in the refrigerator for up to 2 days.

Chorizo and Scrambled Egg Breakfast Tacos

▲▲△

GLUTEN-FREE   NUT-FREE

PREP TIME: 10 minutes / **COOK TIME:** 25 minutes / **TOTAL TIME:** 35 minutes
MAKES: 10 to 12 tacos

This recipe elevates ordinary scrambled eggs by dialing up the flavors with chorizo and lime. You can eat these plain on a plate, or you can heat up tortillas and use the eggs as a filling for delicious breakfast tacos.

1 cup sour cream

1 tablespoon freshly squeezed lime juice

1 teaspoon salt

1 pound ground chorizo

1 medium potato, diced

1 medium onion

½ cup cilantro

6 eggs, beaten

10 to 12 corn tortillas

1 medium tomato, diced

1 cup grated sharp cheddar cheese

1. Mix the sour cream, lime juice, and salt in a bowl and set it aside.

2. In a nonstick sauté pan or skillet, combine the chorizo, potato, onion, and cilantro. Cook for 8 to 10 minutes on medium heat, breaking the chorizo into smaller pieces as it cooks, until the chorizo is browned, the potatoes are tender, and the onions are translucent. Drain the pan of any grease.

3. Reduce the heat to low and add the beaten eggs to the chorizo mixture. Cook slowly for 7 to 10 minutes, stirring occasionally as the eggs bubble, until the eggs are firm but glossy.

4. In a large skillet, heat the flour tortillas, one at a time, until warm.

5. Serve the eggs in the warm tortillas and top them with the sour cream mixture, tomatoes, and cheese.

SUB IN: Try this for the topping instead: one cup of sour cream blended with eight ounces of cream cheese.

spinach soufflé

▲▲▲

NUT-FREE VEGETARIAN

PREP TIME: 15 minutes / **COOK TIME:** 1 hour / **TOTAL TIME:** 1 hour 15 minutes
SERVES: 4

A soufflé takes practice, and this spinach soufflé is a delicious and impressive way to perfect your culinary skills. The key to a soufflé is the egg whites. Whipped egg whites, when cooked, will puff up, causing the soufflé to expand (sometimes over the dish). You'll want to separate your egg yolks from your egg whites completely because the yolks contain fat, and even the smallest bit of yolk will prevent the egg whites from expanding. Beating enough air into the egg whites is also crucial. Be sure to read the tip at the end of this recipe for greater success.

1 (10-ounce) package frozen spinach, thawed

3 egg whites, room temperature, 3 egg yolks reserved

½ teaspoon cream of tartar

3 tablespoons butter

3 tablespoons flour

⅛ teaspoon freshly ground black pepper

2 cups milk

¼ teaspoon salt

1. Preheat the oven to 350°F. Grease an 8-by-8-inch pan. Drain the spinach by placing it in a colander and pressing it with a spoon until all of the liquid is drained.

2. With an electric hand mixer and a metal bowl, beat the egg whites with the cream of tartar for about 5 minutes, or until soft peaks form (when you pull the beaters out of the egg and they make a small "peak" that quickly collapses).

3. Melt the butter in a medium skillet over medium-low heat. Make a roux by slowly whisking in the flour until it creates a paste. Add the black pepper and slowly whisk the milk into the paste. It will begin to thin. Whisk in the reserved egg yolks, one at a time. Stir the drained spinach into the white sauce.

CONTINUED >

4. Fold in the egg whites in three batches: Add ⅓ of the whipped whites to the sauce. Gently fold the whites into the sauce by sliding a spatula under the sauce and along the bottom of the pan, and then folding it up and over the top of the egg whites. Repeat this process two more times until all of the whipped whites are added. Carefully turn the sauce into the prepared pan.

5. Bake on the center rack of the preheated oven for 1 hour. Serve immediately.

PRO TIP: Place a cookie sheet covered with aluminum foil on the bottom rack of your oven. If your soufflé overflows, this will make cleanup easy. Also, no matter how tempting, never open the oven while the soufflé is baking.

HELPFUL HINT: To separate the egg yolks from the whites, carefully crack the eggs (do this over a bowl) and then gently pour the egg from shell half to shell half so that the white falls out and the yolk remains intact. You could also separate an egg yolk in your hands by holding the egg and letting the white run through your fingers, if you don't mind getting messy. Just be sure to wash your hands thoroughly before and after.

Baked Chicken Wings, page 51

CHAPTER THREE

Snacks, Sides, and Drinks

Classic Lemonade

▲△△

DAIRY-FREE   EXTRA QUICK   NUT-FREE   VEGAN

PREP TIME: 5 minutes / **COOK TIME:** 5 minutes / **TOTAL TIME:** 10 minutes
MAKES: 5½ cups, before adding ice

This simple lemonade is the perfect combination of tart and sweet. You'll begin with making your own simple syrup, which is the best way to sweeten cold beverages since solid sugar won't dissolve well in cold liquids. Simple syrup can also be made ahead and stored in your refrigerator for three to four weeks, and it can be used in iced teas, lemonades, and more (try brushing the tops of your cupcakes with simple syrup before icing them to extend their shelf life).

FOR THE SIMPLE SYRUP

3 cups granulated sugar

3 cups water

FOR THE LEMONADE

¾ cup freshly squeezed
    lemon juice

4 cups cold water

Ice

TO MAKE THE SIMPLE SYRUP

1. In a medium saucepan over medium heat, combine the sugar and water and bring it to a boil, frequently stirring to dissolve the sugar. Cover and boil for 5 minutes without stirring. Pour the syrup into a clean, covered jar, and store it in the refrigerator.

TO MAKE THE LEMONADE

2. Combine the simple syrup, lemon juice, and cold water. Add ice to a glass and pour the lemonade over the ice.

> **HELPFUL HINT:** If you don't want to use your stove on a hot summer day, you can substitute ⅔ cup sugar for the simple syrup in this recipe and increase the cold water to 4⅔ cup, stirring until sugar dissolves.

variations:

LIMEADE:

Substitute lime juice for the lemon juice.

RASPBERRY LEMONADE:

Puree 10 ounces of frozen raspberries in a blender with a quarter cup of lemonade. Pour the raspberry mixture into the remaining lemonade and stir.

Grape Rickey

▲△△

DAIRY-FREE EXTRA QUICK NUT-FREE VEGAN

PREP TIME: 5 minutes / **TOTAL TIME:** 5 minutes
MAKES: about 8 cups

My grandmother worked at a soda fountain in the 1940s and liked to make this drink for the soldiers. It's a blend of fruit juices and lemon-lime soda, giving the juice a refreshing twist. There are endless variations you can make by replacing the grape juice with any type of fruit juice you like. Experiment by exchanging the lemon-lime soda for ginger ale, or for a less sweetened version, you can use sparkling water.

4 cups grape juice

6 tablespoons freshly squeezed lime juice

2 tablespoons powdered sugar

3½ cups lemon-lime soda

Ice

1. Combine the fruit juices and the sugar, and then stir until the sugar dissolves. Add the soda.

2. Place ice in glasses and pour the Grape Rickey over the ice to serve.

JAZZ IT UP: You can garnish with fresh fruit or even dip the rim of the glass in water, and then in sugar, for a festive, refreshing beverage.

Sparkling Orange Beverage

▲ △ △

DAIRY-FREE   NUT-FREE   VEGAN

PREP TIME: 1 hour 5 minutes / **TOTAL TIME:** 1 hour 5 minutes

SERVES: 10

· ·

This bright, bubbly drink is great for celebrations or any other day. You can also substitute ⅔ cup of sugar for the simple syrup if you prefer; just stir the drink until the sugar dissolves before putting it in the refrigerator.

2 cups simple syrup
   (see page 38)

2½ cups cold water

16 sprigs mint, chopped

¾ cup freshly squeezed
   orange juice

1 cup freshly squeezed
   lemon juice

4 tablespoons orange zest

2 liters ginger ale

1. In a 2-quart pitcher, combine the simple syrup, water, mint, orange juice, lemon juice, and orange zest. Stir to combine. Chill the juice mixture in the refrigerator for 1 hour, and then strain the liquid (I do this by putting a fine mesh strainer over a second pitcher and pouring from one pitcher into the other).

2. Fill 10 glasses halfway with ice, and then add 5 to 6 tablespoons of the juice mixture to each glass. Top off each glass with the ginger ale.

HELPFUL HINT: You can add the ginger ale directly to the pitcher with the liquid; however, it won't stay bubbly as long. You can also transfer any remaining juice mixture to a jar with a lid and store it in the refrigerator for one week if you don't add the ginger ale directly to it.

Chunky Guacamole

▲△△

DAIRY-FREE EXTRA QUICK GLUTEN-FREE NUT-FREE VEGAN

PREP TIME: 10 minutes / **TOTAL TIME:** 10 minutes

MAKES: 3 cups

This guacamole is a tasty and versatile side. You can serve it as a dip with chips or vegetables, as a salad topping, or set it out for a taco bar. You can add more or less jalapeño or cilantro to appeal to your taste.

½ small onion, chopped

½ teaspoon chopped jalapeño

3 ripe tomatoes, cored and chopped

1 garlic clove, peeled and chopped

½ tablespoon chopped cilantro

3 ripe avocados

½ teaspoon salt

¼ teaspoon freshly ground black pepper

1 tablespoon freshly squeezed lime juice

1. In a bowl, combine the onion, jalapeño, tomato, garlic, and cilantro.

2. Halve the avocados lengthwise and scoop out and discard the pits. Scrape the pulp of the avocado from the skin and add it to the bowl with the tomato mixture. Using a fork, mash the avocado while mixing it with the other ingredients, making a thick, chunky mass. Season with salt and pepper, add the lime juice, and stir to blend.

3. Cover the mixture with plastic wrap and place it in the refrigerator, allowing the flavors to blend for at least 5 minutes before serving.

PRO TIP: To prevent any leftover guacamole from browning, squeeze more lime juice over the top.

Spinach Dip

▲△△

NUT-FREE   VEGETARIAN

PREP TIME: 10 minutes / **COOK TIME:** 25 minutes / **TOTAL TIME:** 35 minutes
SERVES: 6

My mom is an amazing cook, and our dinners were true labors of love growing up. This recipe is one of hers. She fell in love with the spinach dip at a restaurant, and when they declined to give her the recipe, she recreated it on her own at home. You can serve this as a side or as a traditional dip with tortilla strips, chips, crackers, or toast.

3 pounds frozen chopped spinach, thawed and drained

1 pound cream cheese

4 cups shredded cheese (I recommend a mix of Monterey jack and mozzarella)

2 teaspoons hot cayenne powder

½ cup breadcrumbs

1. Preheat the oven to 350°F.

2. Place the spinach, cream cheese, shredded cheese, and cayenne in a bowl. Using an electric hand mixer, or by hand, mix the ingredients in the bowl until well blended. Transfer the mixture to a 13-by-9-inch pan and sprinkle the breadcrumbs on top.

3. Place the pan on the center rack in the preheated oven. Bake for 25 minutes, or until bubbly. Refrigerate any unused dip. It will keep for 3 to 4 days.

PRO TIP: You can also cook this dip in individual portion sizes by placing a serving of the spinach mixture in a microwave-safe bowl, sprinkling it with the breadcrumbs, and heating it in the microwave on high for one minute and 40 seconds or until hot all the way through.

Lexed-Out Waldorf Salad

▲ △ △

GLUTEN-FREE

PREP TIME: 15 minutes, plus at least 1 hour to marinate / **COOK TIME:** 35 minutes / **TOTAL TIME:** 1 hour 50 minutes

SERVES: 6

This salad is an excellent example of how flexible recipes are. Growing up, we'd first go to my maternal grandparents' house for holidays. Their Waldorf salad was a sweet dish made with homemade whipped cream. We would pile it on our plates and feast. Then, we'd go to my paternal grandparents' home and pile their Waldorf salad on our plates, only to remember they make it the traditional way—with mayonnaise. I now live in the South, and my good friend, Alexis, showed me her version, Lexed-Out Waldorf Salad, which includes chicken and a vinaigrette. I'm sharing the Lexed-Out version here with you now. Enjoy!

FOR THE SALAD

¼ cup extra-virgin olive oil

1 teaspoon garlic, chopped

3 tablespoons freshly squeezed lemon juice, divided

2 chicken breasts

2 cups cold water

2 apples, chopped

1 cup spring mix or chopped celery

¼ cup chopped pecans or walnuts

1. Preheat the oven to 350°F.

TO MAKE THE SALAD

2. In a large resealable bag, combine the olive oil, garlic, and 1 tablespoon of the lemon juice. Add the chicken breasts to the bag and allow them to marinate for at least 1 hour but no longer than 6 hours.

3. Bake the chicken on a baking sheet in the preheated oven for 35 minutes, until the internal temperature is 165°F. Cover the baked chicken with aluminum foil and let it rest for 10 minutes, then dice.

4. In a medium mixing bowl, combine the cold water and the remaining 2 tablespoons of lemon juice and stir to blend. Add the apples and allow them to soak for 3 to 5 minutes. Drain and rinse.

¼ cup vinegar (apple cider or rice vinegar)

2 teaspoons Dijon mustard

1 tablespoon honey

¼ teaspoon salt

⅛ teaspoon freshly ground black pepper

¾ cup extra-virgin olive oil

TO MAKE THE VINAIGRETTE

5. While the chicken is in the oven, begin making your dressing. In a medium mixing bowl, combine the vinegar, mustard, honey, salt, and pepper, and then slowly add oil by whisking vigorously or using an immersion blender.

6. In a large bowl, toss the spring mix, apples, and diced chicken and drizzle the salad with the vinaigrette. Top it with the pecans or walnuts and serve.

Corn Casserole

▲△△

PREP TIME: 10 minutes / **COOK TIME:** 1 hour / **TOTAL TIME:** 1 hour 10 minutes
SERVES: 10

When I first tasted this casserole one Thanksgiving at my friend's home, I loved the flavor and texture and had to ask for the recipe. I was delighted to find that the recipe was far easier than I'd imagined. This is a great Thanksgiving side, but it also pairs nicely with most other proteins, including pork, chicken, and beef.

1 (15.25-ounce) can whole kernel corn, with liquid

1 (15.25-ounce) can creamed corn

1 (8.5-ounce) box cornbread mix

¼ cup melted butter

1 cup grated cheddar cheese

1. Preheat the oven to 350°F. Grease an 8-by-8-inch baking pan.

2. In a large mixing bowl, combine the whole-kernel corn, creamed corn, cornbread mix, and butter. Pour the mixture into the prepared baking pan.

3. Place the casserole on the center rack in the preheated oven and bake for 45 minutes. Remove the casserole from the oven and sprinkle it with cheese. Place the casserole back in the oven and bake for 15 minutes, or until the cheese is melted.

PRO TIP: When the timer goes off, insert a butter knife or toothpick in the center of the pan. It will come out clean when the casserole is done.

Spinach Balls

▲△△

NUT-FREE   VEGETARIAN

PREP TIME: 15 minutes / **COOK TIME:** 25 minutes / **TOTAL TIME:** 40 minutes
MAKES: about 40 balls

These spinach balls make a great appetizer or snack. If you want a little more kick, experiment with adding hot sauce or red pepper flakes. These work best if, after forming the balls, you allow them to rest in the refrigerator for about eight hours before baking.

2 (10-ounce) packages frozen chopped spinach, thawed

2 cups dry stuffing mix

4 eggs

1 large onion, grated

¾ cup melted butter

½ cup Parmesan cheese

½ teaspoon garlic salt

½ teaspoon thyme

1. Preheat the oven to 350°F. Lightly grease a cookie sheet.

2. Place the thawed spinach in a colander and mash it with a spoon to release any liquid.

3. In a large mixing bowl, combine the stuffing mix and eggs and mix well with your hands or a large spoon. Add the onion, butter, Parmesan, garlic salt, and thyme and mix well. Using your hands, form the mixture into 2-inch balls. You should get about 40 balls. Place the balls on the prepared cookie sheet.

4. Place the balls in the preheated oven on the center rack and bake for 20 to 25 minutes, or until slightly golden.

> **PRO TIP:** Set out dipping sauces like my Mustard Sauce (page 146), Salsa Lizano (page 153), Tomato Sauce (page 130), or one of your favorite salad dressings to make eating these spinach balls even more fun.

Rustic Focaccia Bread

▲ △ △

`DAIRY-FREE` `EXTRA QUICK` `NUT-FREE` `VEGETARIAN`

PREP TIME: 10 minutes / **COOK TIME:** 30 minutes / **TOTAL TIME:** 45 minutes
SERVES: 6

This bread is fun to make and delicious to eat. Starting with a frozen loaf of bread dough saves time, so you can pack the dough full of rustic Italian flavor with roasted tomatoes, garlic, and rosemary. I love this bread as a snack, but it's also a great side for pastas, soups, and other dishes.

1 (18-ounce) loaf frozen bread dough

¼ cup cornmeal

1½ tablespoons extra-virgin olive oil, divided

1 cup cherry tomatoes, halved

4 garlic cloves, coarsely chopped

2 tablespoons fresh rosemary

1 teaspoon coarse salt

1. Preheat the oven to 375°F. Thaw the bread dough per package instructions. Lightly grease a 13-by-9-inch baking pan. Sprinkle the cornmeal on the bottom of the greased pan.

2. Roll out the bread dough until it's big enough to cover the bottom of the pan. Place the dough in the prepared pan and, using your knuckles, make indentations all over the dough. Brush the indented dough with 1 tablespoon of the olive oil.

3. Heat the remaining ½ tablespoon of olive oil in a medium skillet over medium heat. Add the tomatoes and garlic. Cook for about 6 minutes, occasionally stirring, until the tomatoes blister. Remove the tomatoes from the skillet and place them on top of the dough. Spoon the garlic onto the dough, and then evenly sprinkle the rosemary and coarse salt over the top.

4. Place the pan on the center rack of the preheated oven and bake for 25 minutes, or until the bread is lightly golden brown.

> **JAZZ IT UP:** After brushing the dough with oil, sprinkle with a big pinch (⅛ cup) of Parmesan cheese.

Asparagus with Lemon Dressing

▲△△

DAIRY-FREE   EXTRA QUICK   GLUTEN-FREE   NUT-FREE   VEGETARIAN

PREP TIME: 15 minutes / **COOK TIME:** 5 minutes / **TOTAL TIME:** 20 minutes
SERVES: 5

This asparagus with lemon dressing is best when served at room temperature, but you're also welcome to try it hot or cold. You'll want your asparagus to be tender-crisp, so be careful not to overcook it.

FOR THE ASPARAGUS

2 pounds asparagus

FOR THE LEMON DRESSING

1 egg

3 tablespoons freshly squeezed lemon juice

4 teaspoons English mustard

¼ cup mayonnaise

2 tablespoons white vinegar

⅔ cup extra-virgin olive oil

1 tablespoon lemon zest

1 teaspoon celery seed

⅛ teaspoon sugar

½ teaspoon salt

¼ teaspoon freshly ground black pepper

4 teaspoons finely chopped parsley

TO MAKE THE ASPARAGUS

1. Fill a large bowl with ice water and set it aside.

2. Using a chef's knife, cut off the tough bottom of the stalks of asparagus (about 1½ inches). Pour about 1 inch of water into a large saucepan and bring it to a boil. Lay the asparagus in the boiling water, cover, and cook over medium heat for about 5 minutes, until the stalks are tender but crisp. Remove the asparagus from the saucepan and place them in the prepared bowl of ice water for 2 minutes to immediately stop the cooking process. Then, remove them from the ice water and let them rest and come to room temperature.

TO MAKE THE LEMON DRESSING

3. Combine all of the ingredients, one at a time, whisking briskly after each addition until smooth. Refrigerate the dressing for at least 1 hour (while the asparagus comes to room temperature). Drizzle the dressing over the asparagus and serve. (This makes 1¼ cups of dressing, which can also be used on salads or other vegetables.)

PRO TIP: The lemon dressing keeps well in the refrigerator for up to one week.

Spinach Deviled Eggs

▲△△

DAIRY-FREE EXTRA QUICK GLUTEN-FREE NUT-FREE VEGETARIAN

PREP TIME: 15 minutes / **COOK TIME:** 5 minutes / **TOTAL TIME:** 20 minutes
MAKES: 48 halves

Simple to prepare, deviled eggs are a classic potluck side dish that almost everyone enjoys. This recipe adds spinach for a new twist on the classic deviled egg.

1 (10-ounce) package frozen spinach

24 hard-boiled eggs

1 cup mayonnaise

1 teaspoon salt

½ teaspoon sugar

½ teaspoon celery seeds

½ cup chopped onion

1 teaspoon freshly squeezed lemon juice

½ teaspoon white vinegar

1. Cook the spinach according to the package directions and drain it.

2. Shell the hard-boiled eggs and cut them in half lengthwise. Remove the yolks and place them in a medium mixing bowl. Mash the yolks and combine them with the mayonnaise, salt, sugar, and celery seeds, and mix well.

3. In another medium mixing bowl, combine the spinach, onion, lemon juice, and vinegar. Toss to combine. Add the spinach and yolk mixtures to a blender and blend for about 2 minutes, until smooth and fluffy (you can also use a hand mixer or mix by hand, but the result will not be a smooth, fluffy mixture).

4. Spoon the mixture (or use a piping bag to pipe it) into the cavity of each egg white half. Store the eggs in the refrigerator until ready to serve.

JAZZ IT UP: Sprinkle each deviled egg with about ⅛ teaspoon of regular paprika—or smoked, if you have it!

Baked Chicken Wings

▲△△

DAIRY-FREE   GLUTEN-FREE   NUT-FREE

PREP TIME: 10 minutes / **COOK TIME:** 50 minutes / **TOTAL TIME:** 1 hour
SERVES: 5

....

These chicken wings crisp up in the oven, which makes them a lot easier to cook than fried wings. You can eat them straight out of the oven or toss them in your favorite sauce, like Carolina Barbecue Sauce (page 150). They are delicious hot or cold and make a perfect snack, delicious appetizer, or even a filling meal with a vegetable side.

2 tablespoons extra-virgin olive oil

1 tablespoon kosher salt

½ teaspoon freshly ground black pepper

5 pounds chicken wings (I recommend drumettes)

1. Preheat the oven to 400°F. Wrap a rimmed baking sheet in aluminum foil. If you don't have a rimmed sheet, you will need to place another pan underneath as the wings will drip.

2. In a large mixing bowl, mix together the olive oil, salt, and pepper. Add the chicken wings to the oil mixture and toss them to coat. Place the wings in a single layer on the baking sheet (you may need to do two batches).

3. Place the baking sheet with the chicken on the center rack in the oven and bake for 50 minutes, or until the chicken skin is crispy. Remove them from the oven and toss in your favorite sauce, or enjoy plain.

PRO TIP: For ease in coating the wings in sauce, add the sauce to a gallon resealable bag, and then add some cooked chicken wings, a few at a time, and shake the bag to coat. Remove the coated wings with tongs and repeat.

zucchini Fries

▲△△

PREP TIME: 10 minutes / **COOK TIME:** 20 minutes / **TOTAL TIME:** 30 minutes
SERVES: 2

These taste so great you'd think they were deep-fried instead of baked! Zucchini is a fantastic and healthy alternative to potatoes in this recipe. You may never go back to traditional fries after trying these.

Nonstick cooking spray

1 teaspoon Italian seasoning

½ cup grated Parmesan cheese

1 cup panko breadcrumbs

4 zucchinis, quartered lengthwise

½ cup flour

2 large eggs, beaten

2 tablespoons parsley, freshly chopped

1. Preheat the oven to 425°F, then spray an ovenproof cooling rack with a suitable nonstick spray. Place the cooling rack on a baking sheet.

2. In a medium mixing bowl, combine the Italian seasoning, Parmesan cheese, and panko breadcrumbs.

3. Coat the zucchini quarters in the flour, dip them in the eggs, and then coat them in the seasoned breadcrumbs mixture.

4. Place the zucchini on the prepared baking sheet and bake in the oven for about 20 minutes. Garnish the fries with parsley and serve.

JAZZ IT UP: Give these Zucchini Fries a bit of a kick by adding half a teaspoon of cayenne pepper to the panko mixture.

Ratatouille

▲▲△

DAIRY-FREE NUT-FREE VEGAN

PREP TIME: 15 minutes / **COOK TIME:** 30 minutes / **TOTAL TIME:** 45 minutes
SERVES: 6

Ratatouille is a colorful dish with great flavor and texture, and it makes a satisfying side dish or meatless meal. I love it in the summer and fall, especially when fresh vegetables are more abundant.

½ cup extra-virgin olive oil, divided, plus more if needed

1 onion, chopped fine

2 garlic cloves, minced

1 small eggplant, peeled and cubed

½ cup flour

3 small zucchinis, sliced

3 green bell peppers, seeded and cut into strips

6 ripe tomatoes, peeled, seeded, and chopped

1 teaspoon dried basil

1 teaspoon salt

½ teaspoon freshly ground black pepper

1. Heat ¼ cup of the olive oil in a small skillet over medium heat. Sauté the onion for about 7 minutes, until translucent. Add the garlic and cook for 30 seconds, or until fragrant. Dredge the eggplant in the flour.

2. Heat the remaining ¼ cup of olive oil in a large, ovenproof skillet over medium heat and cook the eggplant for about 10 minutes, until lightly browned. Add more olive oil if necessary. Add the onion and garlic and toss to combine. Add the zucchini, bell peppers, tomatoes, basil, salt, and pepper. Simmer uncovered for about 30 minutes, until the mixture is thick and tender.

HELPFUL HINT: You can add vegetable broth to the leftovers for a hearty vegetable soup. Just add the leftovers to a pot, cover with the broth, and heat until warm.

pumpkin Mashed potatoes

▲▲△

EXTRA QUICK   GLUTEN-FREE   NUT-FREE   VEGETARIAN

PREP TIME: 5 minutes / **COOK TIME:** 25 minutes / **TOTAL TIME:** 30 minutes
MAKES: 4 (¾-cup) servings

This recipe, with its creamy texture of mashed potatoes and earthy flavor of pumpkin, makes a quick side for any meal. These mashed potatoes are delicious on their own, topped with butter, or swimming in your favorite gravy. Garnish this dish with roasted pumpkin seeds for added flair.

3 medium russet potatoes, peeled and quartered

2 garlic cloves, peeled

1 cup canned pumpkin

2 tablespoons cream cheese

1 tablespoon butter

½ teaspoon salt

¼ teaspoon freshly ground black pepper

⅛ teaspoon cinnamon

⅛ teaspoon nutmeg

¼ cup milk

1. Put potatoes and garlic in a large saucepan with enough water to cover them. Bring the pot to a boil and cook for 18 to 20 minutes, or until the potatoes are tender. Turn off the heat and drain the potatoes and garlic in a colander. Return them to the saucepan and mash with a potato masher, or beat them with an electric mixer on low speed until nearly smooth.

2. Beat in the canned pumpkin, cream cheese, butter, salt, pepper, cinnamon, and nutmeg. Gradually add the milk, beating until light and fluffy. Turn the heat back on and heat through.

JAZZ IT UP: Top your mashed potatoes with sprouted pumpkin seeds for added crunch.

Chickpeas with Roasted Vegetables

▲▲△

DAIRY-FREE   GLUTEN-FREE   NUT-FREE   VEGAN

PREP TIME: 10 minutes / **COOK TIME:** 45 minutes / **TOTAL TIME:** 55 minutes
SERVES: 4

This recipe reminds me of dinner at my grandparents' house. They had a garden, and they'd always serve us their garden harvest in some form for dinner. Roasted vegetables were one of my favorites. This recipe adds chickpeas, also known as garbanzo beans, for protein, and the vibrant colors of the dish make a beautiful addition to the plate.

Nonstick cooking spray

5 large carrots, peeled and cut in 2-inch pieces

3 medium sweet potatoes, peeled and cut in chunks

1 large red onion, peeled and cut in 1-inch wedges

3 medium russet potatoes, cubed

6 garlic cloves, minced

1 (16-ounce) can chickpeas, rinsed and drained

2 tablespoons vegetable oil or extra-virgin olive oil

1 teaspoon dried rosemary, crushed

1 teaspoon packed brown sugar

½ teaspoon salt

½ teaspoon freshly ground black pepper

1. Preheat the oven to 425°F. Spray a 13-by-9-inch pan with nonstick spray.

2. Place the carrots, sweet potatoes, onion, russet potatoes, garlic, and chickpeas in the prepared pan.

3. In a small bowl, combine the oil, rosemary, brown sugar, salt, and pepper. Drizzle the oil mixture over the vegetables; toss well to coat.

4. Roast the vegetables in the preheated oven, uncovered, for about 45 minutes, or until the vegetables are lightly browned and tender, stirring twice.

PRO TIP: For the best roasting results, spread the vegetables out on the pan so they're not stacked and are touching each other as little as possible.

German Potato Salad

▲ ▲ ▲

DAIRY-FREE GLUTEN-FREE NUT-FREE

PREP TIME: 15 minutes / **COOK TIME:** 30 minutes / **TOTAL TIME:** 45 minutes
SERVES: 6

This potato salad is versatile. It works great as a hot side, or you can serve it more like traditional potato salad: cold. Either way, it's a crowd-pleaser.

6 to 8 red potatoes

1 thick slice bacon (or 3 slices regular bacon)

2 stalks celery, chopped

¼ cup chopped onion

¾ cup apple cider vinegar

2 tablespoons sugar

1. Scrub the red potatoes, remove any dark spots, and cut them in half. Place the cut potatoes in a large pot and cover with cold water. Over medium-high heat, bring the water to a boil, then reduce the heat to medium and simmer for 15 minutes, or until the potatoes are tender when you push a fork in them. Drain the water from the potatoes. Let them rest while you make the bacon.

2. Dice the bacon, place it in a small sauté pan or skillet over medium heat, and cook for about 8 minutes, until crispy. Remove the pan from the burner and allow it to cool while you finish the potatoes.

3. Slice the potatoes into ½-inch thick slices. Place the potato slices in a large mixing bowl with the celery and onion and toss.

4. Make sure the burner is off and the grease is slightly cooled, then slowly add the vinegar to the pan with the bacon and the grease. Add the sugar and stir for about 3 minutes, until the sugar dissolves in the mixture. Pour the bacon mixture over the potato mixture and toss to coat.

JAZZ IT UP: Garnish this dish with thinly sliced green onion for some added color and a mild oniony flavor.

Baked Tofu Bites

▲ ▲ ▲

DAIRY-FREE   NUT-FREE   VEGAN

PREP TIME: 1 hour / **COOK TIME:** 35 minutes / **TOTAL TIME:** 1 hour 35 minutes
SERVES: 4

These spicy bites make a great vegan dish and are perfect for meatless Mondays. You can drizzle the finished tofu with more hot sauce or serve it as is.

FOR THE TOFU BITES

2 tablespoons hot sauce

2 tablespoons tamari

2 teaspoons English mustard

2 teaspoons onion powder, divided

1 teaspoon garlic powder, divided

¼ teaspoon freshly ground black pepper, plus more for seasoning

15 ounces extra-firm tofu, drained, pressed, and cut into 1-inch cubes

Nonstick cooking spray

3 tablespoons unsweetened plain plant-based milk

½ cup arrowroot powder

1 cup panko breadcrumbs

Pinch salt

TO MAKE THE TOFU BITES

1. In a medium mixing bowl, combine the hot sauce, tamari, mustard, 1 teaspoon of the onion powder, ½ teaspoon of the garlic powder, and the pepper. Stir together until well blended. Add the tofu and gently stir until the tofu cubes are coated. Refrigerate for 1 hour.

2. Preheat the oven to 400°F. Spray a baking sheet with nonstick cooking spray.

3. Remove the cubes from the marinade and add the milk to the remaining marinade. Put the arrowroot powder on a plate. On another large plate, combine the panko breadcrumbs, the remaining teaspoon of onion powder, the remaining ½ teaspoon of garlic powder, and the salt and pepper to taste. Dip the cubes, one at a time, in the milk marinade, shake off any excess liquid, then coat them with the arrowroot. Dip each cube in the milk marinade again, then generously coat it with the panko mixture.

4. Place the coated tofu cubes on the prepared baking sheet and bake for 25 minutes. Turn them over and bake for an additional 10 minutes, until the tofu cubes are a nice golden brown.

CONTINUED >

FOR THE SAUCE

½ cup hot sauce

2 tablespoons vegan
   butter, melted

2 teaspoons
   English mustard

1 teaspoon pure
   maple syrup

1 tablespoon finely
   chopped green onions

TO MAKE THE SAUCE

5. In a medium mixing bowl, whisk the hot sauce, vegan
   butter, mustard, maple syrup, and green onions together.

6. Place toothpicks in each tofu cube and serve with
   the sauce.

PRO TIP: Let the cubed tofu sit on a paper towel for about
five minutes to absorb any excess moisture before adding it to
the bowl.

HELPFUL HINT: To press tofu, place the tofu on a few layers of
paper towels, cover with another paper towel, a cutting board,
and then lay a weight on top of the cutting board (a heavy
bowl or a thick book is a good option). Leave for approximately
30 minutes until the moisture is squeezed out of the tofu.

Boston Baked Beans

▲▲▲

GLUTEN-FREE   NUT-FREE

PREP TIME: 15 minutes / **COOK TIME:** 12 to 14 hours / **TOTAL TIME:** 12 hours 15 minutes
SERVES: 6

Boston baked beans are a tasty dish where the beans caramelize in their juices. It's a wonderful and easy way to cook, with no soaking or fussing. This is a dump and go recipe. I recommend using a slow-cooker; however, you can also make these in the oven in a large pot. Cooking beans from scratch is a great cooking skill. These beans take a full day to cook, with minimal supervision, but they are worth the wait. Typically, Boston tradition is to serve these beans on a Saturday night with a side of coleslaw and Boston brown bread.

1 (2-inches-thick, 6- to 8-ounce, square) piece salt pork

2 quarts water

2 cups small white beans, well picked over and washed

5 cups water

1½ teaspoons salt

1 cup finely sliced onion

2 large garlic cloves, minced

2 tablespoons dark molasses

2 tablespoons English mustard

½ teaspoon dried thyme

2 bay leaves

½ tablespoon grated ginger

½ teaspoon freshly ground black pepper

1. Cut the salt pork into ⅜-inch-thick strips (leave on the rind). In a large pot, bring 2 quarts of water to a simmer. Add the pork strips and simmer for 10 minutes (don't worry if the pork looks the same; it isn't going to change much). Drain, then rinse the pork in cold water and add to a large slow cooker or ovenproof pot.

2. Add the beans, water, salt, onion, garlic, molasses, mustard, thyme, bay leaves, ginger, and pepper to the pot with the salt pork and bring to a simmer. Cook over low heat (preheated 250°F oven or slow cooker) for 12 to 14 hours. The beans should barely bubble. Check on and stir the beans regularly. You may need to add boiling water if they become too thick. They are done when they are soft and have turned a dark, reddish brown.

scalloped potatoes

▲▲▲

GLUTEN-FREE NUT-FREE VEGETARIAN

PREP TIME: 20 minutes / **COOKING TIME:** 1 hour 20 minutes /
TOTAL TIME: 1 hour 40 minutes

SERVES: 6

These tender potatoes enveloped in a creamy white sauce are one of my favorite recipes. Boiling the potatoes directly in the cream adds starch from the potatoes that helps thicken the sauce. A final bake in the oven finishes thickening up the cream and browns the top for a delicious side dish.

1½ cups heavy (whipping) cream

2 cups half-and-half

1 large garlic clove, minced

½ teaspoon salt

¼ teaspoon freshly ground black pepper

1 bay leaf

2 pounds red or Yukon Gold potatoes

½ cup grated cheddar cheese

1. Pour the cream and half-and-half into a large saucepan. Stir in the garlic, salt, pepper, and bay leaf. Over medium-low heat, begin heating the cream mixture.

2. Slice the potatoes about ⅛ inch thick. Drop the sliced potatoes into the cream as you slice them. When all the potatoes are in the cream, the surface of the cream mixture should be ½ inch above the potatoes (if not, add more cream until it's ½ inch above the potatoes).

3. Bring the cream and potatoes to just below the simmering point and maintain for 1 hour, or until the potatoes are tender. Check the cream frequently to be sure it's not boiling (this will cause your cream to curdle). Stir occasionally to keep the potatoes from sticking to the bottom of the pan and scorching.

4. Place an oven rack in the top position and preheat the oven to 425°F. Butter a 9-by-13-inch baking dish.

5. When the potatoes are tender, turn them into prepared baking dish. Sprinkle them with the cheese and bake for 20 minutes, or until bubbling and lightly browned on top. The potatoes should be dry rather than mushy.

**Prosciutto and Pear
Sandwich, page 77**

CHAPTER FOUR

Cooking for Yourself

Avocado Toast

▲△△

DAIRY-FREE **EXTRA QUICK** **NUT-FREE** **VEGAN**

PREP TIME: 5 minutes / **TOTAL TIME:** 5 minutes
SERVES: 1

This is an easy meal or snack with minimal ingredients and endless possibilities. Experiment with varieties of bread for different textures. You can add a fried egg or top it with cheese, bean sprouts, spinach—whatever suits your taste buds.

½ ripe avocado
¼ teaspoon salt
1 slice bread, toasted

1. Remove the pit from the avocado half and use a spoon to scoop out the avocado and place it in a small bowl. Using a fork, mash the avocado to the texture you like (smooth or chunky). Add the salt and mix until combined.

2. Spread the mashed avocado on your toast.

JAZZ IT UP: Stir two tablespoons of salsa into the mashed avocado before spreading it on the toast for some added spice and zing.

Fruit Nachos

▲△△

EXTRA QUICK · GLUTEN-FREE · VEGETARIAN

PREP TIME: 5 minutes / **COOK TIME:** 10 seconds / **TOTAL TIME:** 5 minutes 10 seconds
SERVES: 1

Fruit nachos make an ideal after-school snack. I've included two versions here: one with a delicious peanut butter sauce, and one with a refreshing yogurt sauce. Either way, it's an excellent dish you can make with any type of fruit that's in season.

FOR THE NACHOS

2 cups fruit, sliced (try apples, peaches, apricots, berries, or bananas)

FOR THE YOGURT SAUCE

1 cup plain Greek yogurt

1 tablespoon freshly squeezed lemon or orange juice

1 teaspoon vanilla extract

FOR THE PEANUT BUTTER SAUCE

1 cup peanut butter

TOPPINGS (OPTIONAL)

Pumpkin or sunflower seeds

Chocolate chips

Dried fruit

Nuts

TO MAKE THE NACHOS

1. Arrange your fresh fruit on a serving plate.

TO MAKE THE YOGURT SAUCE

2. In a small bowl, combine the yogurt, juice, and vanilla and whisk until well combined. Drizzle the yogurt sauce over the fruit and sprinkle it with your chosen toppings.

TO MAKE THE PEANUT BUTTER SAUCE

3. Place peanut butter in a microwave-safe container and heat it in the microwave for 10 seconds. Whisk the sauce until smooth, drizzle it over the fruit, and then sprinkle with your chosen toppings.

> **PRO TIP:** You can make the yogurt mixture ahead of time and store it in the refrigerator for up to three days, making it easy to make these fruit nachos whenever you like.

Tofu Tostadas

▲ △ △

DAIRY-FREE **EXTRA QUICK** **NUT-FREE** **VEGAN**

PREP TIME: 10 minutes / **COOK TIME:** 5 minutes / **TOTAL TIME:** 15 minutes
MAKES: 2 tostadas

It's been a decade since my son introduced our family to tofu. My younger kids still remember these tofu tostadas he would make for them and occasionally ask for them. They are light, tasty, and incredibly easy to make.

¼ pound extra firm tofu

1 tablespoon extra-virgin olive oil

2 tablespoons finely chopped onion

1 small Roma tomato, diced

1 small avocado, peeled, pitted, and diced

1 tablespoon cilantro

2 tablespoons freshly squeezed lime juice

2 crispy tostada shells

1. Drain the tofu and cut it into 1-inch chunks.

2. In a medium sauté pan or skillet over medium-low heat, add the oil and tofu and cook for 5 minutes, frequently stirring. The tofu will become a light golden color.

3. Add the tofu to a medium mixing bowl along with the onion, tomato, avocado, cilantro, and lime juice. Toss to mix.

4. Top each tostada shell with half of the tofu mixture and serve.

JAZZ IT UP: Chopped cabbage or shredded lettuce make an awesome addition to this dish. You can add them to the mixing bowl when you toss everything else.

Mango Salad with Basil Dressing

▲△△

DAIRY-FREE **EXTRA QUICK** **GLUTEN-FREE** **VEGETARIAN (OPTIONAL)**

PREP TIME: 10 minutes / **TOTAL TIME:** 10 minutes

MAKES: 4 cups

Fresh ingredients make this mango salad a refreshing snack or light meal. You can add diced chicken or steak if you like or experiment with exchanging the mango for blueberries, pineapple, chunks of Granny Smith apples, or papaya. It's also delicious garnished with shredded coconut.

FOR THE MANGO SALAD

4 cups chopped lettuce

1 carrot, shredded

1 red bell pepper, diced

1 cucumber, diced

1 mango, peeled, pitted, and cubed

FOR THE BASIL DRESSING

1 cup basil

3 teaspoons freshly squeezed lime juice

1 scallion, chopped

1 teaspoon soy sauce or fish sauce

1 garlic clove

2 teaspoons sugar

TOPPING

½ cup dry roasted peanuts or cashews

TO MAKE THE MANGO SALAD

1. Place the lettuce, carrot, bell pepper, and cucumber in a large bowl. Add the mango to the vegetables.

TO MAKE THE BASIL DRESSING

2. Blend the basil, lime juice, scallion, soy sauce, garlic, and sugar in a blender until semiliquid (it will be chunky from the basil).

3. Drizzle the dressing over the mango salad and toss to coat. Top with the nuts.

SUB IN: For a unique and sweet spin, you can substitute raisins for the peanuts.

Ricotta and Spinach Pizza

▲ △ △

EXTRA QUICK   NUT-FREE   VEGETARIAN

PREP TIME: 5 minutes / **COOK TIME:** 15 minutes / **TOTAL TIME:** 20 minutes
MAKES: 1 small pizza

You'll use a premade crust in this recipe as a shortcut to this delicious pizza. You can even use the topping here for my French Bread Pizza (page 74). Feel free to use additional toppings such as black olives, sliced bell pepper, or crumbled cooked bacon, for a non-veggie spin.

2 tablespoons butter

2 tablespoons onion, finely chopped

2 tablespoons garlic, chopped

1 pound fresh baby spinach, divided

1 cup ricotta cheese

1 ready-to-bake premade pizza crust

6 cherry tomatoes, halved (optional)

1. Preheat the oven to 450°F.

2. In a medium skillet over medium-high heat, melt the butter. Add the onion and sauté for about 3 minutes, until translucent. Add the garlic and stir until fragrant. Set aside and reserve one cup of spinach; add the rest to the skillet and sauté for about 4 minutes, until it begins to wilt.

3. Spread the ricotta cheese over the pizza crust. Spread out the reserved 1 cup of spinach on top of the ricotta. Top the pizza with the sautéed vegetables and cherry tomato halves (if using).

4. Bake the pizza in the preheated oven for 10 minutes, or until the crust is crunchy. You can set the pizza directly on the oven rack with an aluminum foil pan on the oven rack below to catch any drippings.

JAZZ IT UP: For an even cheesier pizza, spread a quarter cup of shredded mozzarella cheese on top of the pizza before you put it in the oven.

submarine sandwich

▲△△

EXTRA QUICK   NUT-FREE

PREP TIME: 5 minutes / TOTAL TIME: 5 minutes
MAKES: 1 sandwich

The great thing about a submarine sandwich is you can customize the ingredients to make it a meal you want to sink your teeth into. This recipe is just a general outline for making a sandwich, so feel free to swap out the deli meats for ones you prefer and add or omit toppings as you like.

1 submarine roll

2 tablespoons mayonnaise

½ teaspoon salt

½ teaspoon freshly ground black pepper

2 tablespoons vinaigrette dressing

2 (4-ounce) slices ham

2 (4-ounce) slices salami

4 slices Swiss cheese

1 medium tomato, sliced

½ cup shredded lettuce

1. Open or cut the submarine roll in half lengthwise.

2. Spread each bread half with 1 tablespoon of mayonnaise. You can add other condiments such as mustard, too.

3. Sprinkle on the salt and pepper and drizzle with the vinaigrette dressing.

4. Layer the ham, salami, and cheese on top of the bread. Top with slices of tomato and the lettuce. Close the sandwich and enjoy!

JAZZ IT UP: You can toast the bread before adding your toppings. I like to spread each bread half with butter (about one tablespoon total), place them butter-side up on a cookie sheet, and then toast them under a preheated broiler for two minutes. Be sure to keep a close eye on them to make sure they don't burn.

Bean Burritos

▲△△

PREP TIME: 10 minutes / **COOK TIME:** 15 minutes / **TOTAL TIME:** 25 minutes
MAKES: 3 burritos

For this recipe, we'll start with classic bean burritos, and in the variation I'll show you how to add ground beef, if you'd like. You can also sprinkle on any toppings you choose to customize your burrito.

1 (16-ounce) can refried beans

3 (8-inch) tortillas

3 tablespoons salsa, or Salsa Lizano (page 153)

¼ cup diced onion

½ cup shredded cheddar cheese

1. Heat the refried beans in a small saucepan over low heat for about 5 minutes, stirring occasionally, until you can easily stir them.

2. In a medium skillet over low heat, warm the tortillas for 30 seconds on each side (they may begin to blister).

3. Top each tortilla with ⅓ of the beans. Add the salsa, shredded cheese, and onions along with any other toppings. Fold the tortilla sides over the filling and tightly roll up the burrito.

PRO TIP: For a more taco-packed flavor, add half a tablespoon of taco seasoning to the refried beans while you're heating them up.

Burrito Variation:

GROUND BEEF AND BEAN BURRITO:

In a small skillet over medium heat, cook a quarter pound of ground beef with the onions for about 7 minutes, until the onions are translucent and the ground beef is browned. Drain the grease from the skillet and return it to the stove. Add the can of refried beans and stir for about 5 minutes, until the beans and ground beef are well combined. Then, proceed with the final two steps of my Bean Burrito recipe.

Cheesy Pigs-in-a-Blanket Rollups

▲△△

EXTRA QUICK   NUT-FREE

PREP TIME: 10 minutes / **COOK TIME:** 12 minutes / **TOTAL TIME:** 25 minutes
MAKES: 8 mini hot dogs

These rollups make a fun meal. Serve them with your favorite hot dog condiments and dip them as you eat. You'll have dough left over, so I've included instructions for making cinnamon triangles that bake along with the hot dogs for a sweet treat!

FOR THE PIGS-IN-A-BLANKET

Nonstick cooking spray

1 (8-ounce) can refrigerated crescent rolls

½ cup grated cheddar cheese

4 hot dogs (turkey or beef)

FOR THE CINNAMON TRIANGLES (OPTIONAL)

Leftover crescent roll dough

1 to 2 tablespoons melted butter

1 tablespoon cinnamon

1 tablespoon sugar

TO MAKE THE PIGS-IN-A-BLANKET

1. Preheat the oven to 425°F. Spray a baking sheet with nonstick spray.

2. Unroll the can of crescent rolls and carefully separate the dough on the perforations to create triangles. Add one tablespoon of the grated cheese to the center of the wide end of each triangle.

3. Cut the hot dogs in half crosswise (so you have 8 small hot dog pieces). Place each hot dog piece at the wide end of a dough triangle. Roll the dough to the short end and pinch to seal the overlap. Repeat with all the hot dogs.

TO MAKE THE CINNAMON TRIANGLES

4. With the leftover dough, spread each triangle with a light coat of butter and sprinkle them with cinnamon and sugar.

5. Place the rolled hot dogs and cinnamon triangles (if making) on the prepared baking sheet and bake in the preheated oven for 12 minutes, or until the dough is a golden brown.

Chicken Nugget Sliders

▲△△

EXTRA QUICK   NUT-FREE

PREP TIME: 5 minutes / **COOK TIME:** 10 minutes / **TOTAL TIME:** 15 minutes
MAKES: 2 sliders

These chicken nugget sliders are so simple to throw together that one of my sons has been making them since he was five. My husband eats them by the handful. They are easy to make whether you want one or ten!

2 white meat
   chicken nuggets

1 (2-ounce) slice
   cheddar cheese

2 slider buns

1 leaf lettuce

2 tomato slices

1. Preheat the toaster oven to 350°F. Cover a toaster oven tray with aluminum foil.

2. Place nuggets on the prepared tray and lay half of the cheese slice on top of each nugget. Bake them in the preheated toaster oven for 10 minutes.

3. Remove the nuggets from the toaster oven, open the slider buns, and add half of the lettuce leaf and a tomato slice to each bun. Add one nugget to prepared slider bun and enjoy. Try serving them with your favorite dipping sauce!

HELPFUL HINT: To make these sliders in the microwave, arrange the frozen nuggets on a microwave-safe plate, top each nugget with half of the cheese slice, and heat them on high for 30 seconds. Assemble them as directed in the final instruction.

JAZZ IT UP: For a buffalo chicken-style slider, add a tablespoon of buffalo hot sauce to each nugget after they're warmed. I like to use blue cheese or ranch dressing as a dipping sauce when I make them this way.

French Bread Pizza

▲△△

EXTRA QUICK   NUT-FREE

PREP TIME: 5 minutes / **COOK TIME:** 12 minutes / **TOTAL TIME:** 20 minutes
SERVES: 2

This is the perfect go-to recipe when you want to entertain your friends or just make a quick meal to feed yourself. The base of this pizza is a loaf of French bread, though you can also substitute a loaf of Italian bread for the crust. You'll create your personal pizza by adding sauce, cheese, and your choice of toppings.

1 French bread loaf

1 (14-ounce) jar pizza sauce

1 cup shredded Mozzarella cheese

1 (6-ounce) package sliced pepperoni

TOPPINGS (OPTIONAL)

Browned sausage

Olives

Green peppers

Shredded chicken

Mushrooms

1. Preheat the oven to 400°F. Cover a baking sheet with aluminum foil for easy cleanup.

2. Cut the loaf of bread in half lengthwise. Place the bread, cut-sides up, on the prepared baking sheet.

3. Spread the pizza sauce on the bread slices. Sprinkle the sauce with the cheese. Top the cheese with pepperoni or other chosen toppings.

4. Place the baking sheet with prepared pizzas on the center rack in the preheated oven. Bake for 12-minutes, or until the cheese melts.

JAZZ IT UP: Don't limit yourself to just these toppings. Most any pizza topping you love will do. Even anchovies if that's your thing!

Tofu Burger

▲△△

DAIRY-FREE   EXTRA QUICK   NUT-FREE   VEGAN

PREP TIME: 10 minutes / **COOK TIME:** 15 minutes / **TOTAL TIME:** 25 minutes
MAKES: 1 burger

One of my sons started making these tofu burgers when he decided to live a vegan lifestyle. He was generous and made enough for his younger siblings, who thought they were something spectacular. You can eat this flavorful burger plain or place the patty between two slices of your favorite bread and garnish the burger with the toppings of your choice.

¼ pound extra firm tofu

1 tablespoon whole wheat flour

1 tablespoon fine cornmeal

1 tablespoon quick oats

⅛ cup fresh basil leaves

¼ teaspoon paprika

¼ teaspoon cumin

⅛ teaspoon dried thyme

⅛ teaspoon ginger

⅛ teaspoon salt

1 drop hot sauce

1 tablespoon extra-virgin olive oil

¼ teaspoon crushed garlic

1. Cut the tofu into 1-inch chunks and mash them by hand or with a food processor. Add the flour, cornmeal, oats, basil, paprika, cumin, thyme, ginger, salt, and hot sauce, and blend on low in the processor or by hand until the mixture begins to clump. Form the tofu mixture into a 4-inch patty.

2. Heat the olive oil in a medium, nonstick sauté pan or skillet over medium heat. Add the garlic and stir just until fragrant. Add the patty to the oil and cook for 7 minutes on each side, or until golden brown.

JAZZ IT UP: Treat this like you might a beef or turkey burger. Use all of your favorite burger toppings or experiment with others to see what works best with the flavors that pop in this one.

Hot Ham Sandwiches

▲△△

EXTRA QUICK   NUT-FREE

PREP TIME: 5 minutes / **COOK TIME:** 5 minutes / **TOTAL TIME:** 10 minutes
MAKES: 2 sandwiches

These hot ham sandwiches are a great way to use leftover ham. This recipe shows you how to heat it up, but it's equally as good cold; just skip buttering the buns, pile on the filling, and feast! You can also double or quadruple the recipe, wrap leftover sandwiches individually in aluminum foil, and heat them up later for a great anytime snack.

2 sandwich buns

2 tablespoons
butter, softened

¼ pound cooked
ham, chopped

2 tablespoons grated
Swiss cheese

1 hard-boiled egg, chopped

1 tablespoon sweet
pickle relish

2 tablespoons finely
chopped onion

⅛ cup mayonnaise

1. Preheat the oven to 375°F. Butter the buns.

2. In a small mixing bowl, combine the ham, Swiss cheese, egg, pickle relish, onion, and mayonnaise and mix until well-blended.

3. Spoon the mixture onto the buttered buns, assemble the sandwiches, and wrap them with foil. Place the sandwiches in the preheated oven for 5 minutes, or until heated through.

HELPFUL HINT: You can make more of this filling, prepare several sandwiches at once, and then freeze them. To warm the frozen sandwiches, heat them in the oven at 350°F for 10 to 15 minutes, or until thawed and warmed through.

Prosciutto and Pear Sandwich

▲△△

EXTRA QUICK   NUT-FREE

PREP TIME: 5 minutes / **TOTAL TIME:** 5 minutes
MAKES: 1 sandwich

The flavors of this sandwich are both sweet and savory. You can spread your favorite condiments on this sandwich, and fresh spring greens are also a delicious addition.

1 medium pear,
   thinly sliced

1 tablespoon apple
   cider vinegar

2 slices sourdough bread

1 tablespoon blackberry
   or strawberry
   preserves (optional)

4 slices prosciutto

1 (2-ounce) slice
   cheddar cheese

1. Place the pear slices in a small bowl and add the apple cider vinegar. Toss to coat the pear slices and let them rest for 2 minutes.

2. In a toaster, toast the sourdough bread.

3. Add any condiments to your bread slices, such as the preserves (if using) or more savory options like mayonnaise or mustard. Then, top them with the pear, prosciutto, and cheese. Place the second slice of bread on top and serve.

SUB IN: You can substitute Granny Smith apple for the pear, and I encourage you to experiment with replacing the apple cider vinegar with orange juice, grape juice, or lemon juice for different flavors.

Scrambled Eggs with Chili Sauce

▲△△

EXTRA QUICK GLUTEN-FREE NUT-FREE VEGETARIAN

PREP TIME: 5 minutes / **COOK TIME:** 5 minutes / **TOTAL TIME:** 10 minutes
SERVES: 1

My grandmother made an amazing chili sauce, which I loved mixed in with my eggs. This recipe will walk you through making basic scrambled eggs, and then we'll take a short cut by using a bottled chili sauce rather than my Grandma Jana's Chili Sauce (page 152). It's still delicious. Try serving these with my Pan-Fried Sausages and Potatoes (page 83).

FOR THE SCRAMBLED EGGS

2 eggs

⅓ cup milk

¼ teaspoon salt

⅛ teaspoon freshly ground black pepper

2 tablespoons butter

FOR THE CHILI SAUCE

1 tablespoon melted butter

3 tablespoons chili sauce

½ teaspoon minced onion

TO MAKE THE SCRAMBLED EGGS

1. In a small mixing bowl, quickly beat the eggs, and then add the milk, salt, and pepper and beat thoroughly.

2. Melt the butter in a small skillet over medium-low heat. Pour the egg mixture into the skillet and cook for about 5 minutes, until thick and creamy, occasionally scraping the egg mixture from the bottom and sides of the pan as it sets.

TO MAKE THE CHILI SAUCE

3. Combine the melted butter, chili sauce, and onion in a small bowl. When the eggs start to set, quickly stir the chili sauce mixture into the eggs.

JAZZ IT UP: The omelet recipe variations (see page 17) work well here. Just use the toppings from those here in step 1 and make the scrambled eggs as instructed.

Ground Beef Nachos

▲△△

EXTRA QUICK   NUT-FREE

PREP TIME: 15 minutes / **COOK TIME:** 20 minutes / **TOTAL TIME:** 35 minutes
MAKES: 1 large plate of nachos

In this recipe, you'll make an ooey-gooey cheese sauce to spoon over hot tortilla chips, and then you'll pile them high with ground beef and your choice of toppings to make these nachos all about your taste! These nachos are big on flavor and an easy meal.

¼ pound ground beef

½ teaspoon salt

4 ounces cream cheese, cubed

¼ cup grated cheddar cheese

1 cup grated jalapeño cheese

4 tablespoons chunky salsa

¼ cup milk

20 to 30 tortilla chips

TOPPINGS (OPTIONAL)

Diced tomatoes

Jalapeño slices

Black olives

Sliced avocado

Chopped cilantro

Salsa

Freshly squeezed lime juice

1. Preheat the oven to 350°F.

2. In a small sauté pan or skillet over medium heat, cook the ground beef for about 8 minutes, until brown. Drain, stir in the salt, and set aside.

3. In a small saucepan over medium-low heat, combine the cream cheese, cheddar cheese, jalapeño cheese, and salsa and melt for about 7 minutes. Whisk in the milk to thin the sauce.

4. Place the chips on a baking sheet and bake in the preheated oven for 5 minutes. Transfer the chips to a plate, spoon the ground beef over the chips, drizzle with the cheese sauce, and add your desired toppings.

PRO TIP: When you're in the mood for a really quick snack, you can make super easy and basic cheese nachos by placing the tortilla chips on a microwave-safe plate, adding 1¼ cup of shredded cheddar cheese, and microwaving the nachos on high for 20 seconds, or until the cheese is melted.

Chicken Fried Steak

▲▲△

EXTRA QUICK | NUT-FREE

PREP TIME: 5 minutes / **COOK TIME:** 10 minutes / **TOTAL TIME:** 15 minutes
SERVES: 1

I loved chicken fried steak growing up, and my children share that same love. It's a steak dredged in flour and milk, then fried to a crisp golden brown. The oil is then used to make a delicious milk gravy to pour over the steak. Try these served with Pumpkin Mashed Potatoes (see page 54).

FOR THE STEAK

2 tablespoons all-purpose flour

½ teaspoon salt

½ teaspoon freshly ground black pepper

1 tablespoon milk

1 large cube steak

6 tablespoons shortening

FOR THE MILK GRAVY

1 tablespoon reserved melted shortening

1 tablespoon flour

1 cup milk

½ teaspoon salt

½ teaspoon freshly ground black pepper

TO MAKE THE STEAK

1. In a medium mixing bowl, combine the flour, salt, and black pepper and stir to combine. Pour the milk in another small bowl. Dredge the steak in the milk, and then dip it in the flour mixture to coat all sides.

2. In a small skillet (wide enough for your steak to lay flat in) over medium heat, melt the shortening for 2 minutes. Once the shortening is hot, add the floured steak to the skillet and cook for 2 minutes, or until lightly browned. Turn the steak over and cook the other side for 2 minutes, or until lightly browned.

TO MAKE THE MILK GRAVY

3. Once the steak is browned, set it aside. Reserve 1 tablespoon of the melted shortening and drain the remaining liquid from the pan. Stir in the fresh flour and whisk for about 1 minute to make a thick paste. Make sure you scrape up and mix in any stuck-on bits from the pan to add to the flavor. Whisk in the milk until smooth and add the salt and pepper. Continuously whisk for about 3 minutes, or until the gravy is thickened to your liking.

Turkey and Fried Egg Sandwich

▲▲△

EXTRA QUICK   NUT-FREE

PREP TIME: 5 minutes / **COOK TIME:** 10 minutes / **TOTAL TIME:** 15 minutes
MAKES: 1 sandwich

This is the ultimate turkey sandwich, topped with a fried egg and complemented by a smoky chipotle sauce. You can make it cold (with a warm fried egg), but I like it best as a sandwich melt, which is how I designed this recipe.

FOR THE CHIPOTLE MAYONNAISE

2 tablespoons mayonnaise

1 tablespoon sour cream

1 teaspoon freshly squeezed lime juice

¼ teaspoon chipotle powder

FOR THE SANDWICH

1 tablespoon butter

2 slices sourdough bread (optional)

2 tablespoons chipotle mayonnaise

2 (4-ounce) slices smoked turkey

2 (2-ounce) slices Gruyère cheese

3 tablespoons vegetable oil, divided

1 medium egg

½ cup spinach

TO MAKE THE CHIPOTLE MAYONNAISE

1. Place the mayonnaise, sour cream, lime juice, and chipotle powder in a small bowl and mix until well combined.

TO MAKE THE SANDWICH

2. Butter one side of each slice of bread. Place the bread, buttered-side down, in a large skillet over medium-low heat. Spread the unbuttered side of the bread slices with the chipotle mayonnaise. Top the bread with the turkey and cheese. Cover the pan and cook for 5 minutes, or until the cheese begins to melt. During this time, you can cook your egg.

3. Heat 2 tablespoons of the vegetable oil in a small skillet over medium-low heat for about 1 minute. Break the egg into a saucer and carefully slip the egg into the oil. Reduce the heat to low and cook until the white is partially set. Gently slide a spatula under the egg and carefully flip the egg. Cook for about 2 more minutes. Lift the cover from the pan with the bread slices and use a spatula to slide the egg onto one slice of the bread.

CONTINUED >

4. Return the egg pan to the burner over low heat, then add the spinach and the remaining 1 tablespoon of vegetable oil. Stir for about 3 minutes, until the spinach is wilted and soft. Add the spinach on top of the egg.

5. Gently slide a spatula under the slice of bread without the egg and turn it over onto the egg side. Cover the pan and cook for 1 minute. Transfer the sandwich to a plate and enjoy!

PRO TIP: For the best experience, your egg should be a little over medium with a runny yolk and firm whites. I recommend cooking it for about three minutes per side.

Pan-Fried Sausages and Potatoes

▲▲△

DAIRY-FREE   GLUTEN-FREE   NUT-FREE

PREP TIME: 10 minutes / **COOK TIME:** 35 minutes / **TOTAL TIME:** 45 minutes

SERVES: 1

Pork sausage should be cooked well done, or until it loses any pink color and is nicely browned. We'll walk through two different ways to panfry sausages, and you can try one or both. Paired with crispy potatoes, this makes a great meal. You can even add an egg to complement the dish.

FOR THE SAUSAGES

2 Italian sausage links

FOR THE POTATOES

2 tablespoons shortening

¼ cup sliced onions (optional)

2 cups potatoes, cut into ¼-inch-thick slices

½ teaspoon salt

¼ teaspoon freshly ground black pepper

TO MAKE THE SAUSAGES

1. **Use the steam method:** Place the links in a small skillet and half-cover them with warm water. Cover the skillet and let the sausages steam over low heat for 5 minutes. Drain the water and continue cooking the links over low heat, frequently turning, until plump and browned.

2. *Or* use the pan method: In a small cold skillet over low heat, cook the sausages for 12 to 14 minutes, frequently turning to brown. Drain the fat as it accumulates.

TO MAKE THE POTATOES

3. Heat the shortening in a large, covered skillet. Add the onions (if using) and potatoes and sprinkle with the salt and pepper. Sauté, covered, over low heat for 15 minutes. Then, remove the lid, increase the heat to medium, and sauté for 10 minutes more, or until the potatoes are brown and crusty, turning occasionally.

> **HELPFUL HINT:** Be sure to wear long oven mitts when working with hot shortening or any grease in a pan.

Fish Chowder

▲▲△

EXTRA QUICK GLUTEN-FREE NUT-FREE

PREP TIME: 5 minutes / **COOK TIME:** 25 minutes / **TOTAL TIME:** 30 minutes
MAKES: about 4 cups

Fish chowder made from scratch is easier than you'd think. This makes one big bowl. Eat it all or store the leftovers in an airtight container in the refrigerator to finish the next day. It's especially delicious topped with oyster crackers. Salt pork renders fat that makes the flavor of the fish stand out without overpowering the dish, and it adds a salty, smoky flavor.

1 (2-ounce, 1½-inch-thick) piece salt pork, cubed

1 small onion, coarsely chopped

1 cup water

2 potatoes, cut into 1¼-inch-long and ⅜-inch-thick strips

1 cup chicken broth

1 pound cod

2 cups milk

¼ teaspoon freshly ground black pepper

1 tablespoon butter

1. In a medium skillet over medium heat, sauté the salt pork until it's golden brown and crispy. Remove the pieces that are mostly pork (rather than mostly fat) from the skillet. To the salt-pork fat left in the skillet, add the onion and sauté for 7 minutes, until translucent.

2. In the same skillet over medium-high heat, bring the water to a boil. Once it's boiling, add the potato strips and continue boiling for 5 minutes. Add the chicken broth and cod and simmer uncovered for 10 minutes, or until the fish is done. Add the milk, pepper, and butter and heat until the butter melts.

JAZZ IT UP: Thinly slice two small carrots and add them to the pan alongside the onion and the pork.

Pad Thai Noodle Salad

▲▲△

DAIRY-FREE EXTRA QUICK GLUTEN-FREE

PREP TIME: 15 minutes / **COOK TIME:** 5 minutes / **TOTAL TIME:** 20 minutes
MAKES: 1 large salad

Thai food is full of flavors, and this dish offers rice noodles, plenty of vegetables, and shrimp. It's all topped with a chili sauce, which you can adjust to make the salad sweeter or spicier.

FOR THE DRESSING

1½ tablespoons tamarind paste

½ cup boiling water

¼ cup sugar

¼ cup soy sauce or fish sauce

2 tablespoons chili sauce

FOR THE NOODLE SALAD

4 ounces rice noodles

10 to 15 uncooked shrimp

2 tablespoons vegetable oil

½ teaspoon freshly grated ginger

2 garlic cloves

½ jalapeño, thinly sliced

2 scallions, thinly sliced

½ bell pepper, julienned

¼ cup chopped celery

1 cup bean sprouts

½ cup cilantro

2 tablespoons dry-roasted peanuts

TO MAKE THE DRESSING

1. In a small mixing bowl, combine the tamarind paste and boiling water and stir until the paste is fully dissolved. Add the sugar, soy sauce, and chili sauce to the mixture and stir well to dissolve the sugar and blend the flavors. Taste the dressing—add more sugar for a sweeter dressing or more chili sauce for a dressing with more spice.

TO MAKE THE NOODLE SALAD

2. Prepare the rice noodles per the package instructions, then drain them. Rinse the cooked noodles with cold water and drain again.

3. In a small bowl, pour ¼ of the dressing on top of the shrimp.

4. Heat the vegetable oil in a medium skillet over medium heat. Add the ginger and garlic and cook for 1 minute, or until fragrant. Add the shrimp and cook for 3 minutes, or until the shrimp turn pink.

5. Transfer the shrimp to a serving bowl and toss with the cooked noodles. Garnish the salad with the jalapeño, scallions, celery, bean sprouts, cilantro, and peanuts and top with the rest of the dressing.

Cuban-Inspired Pork Sandwich

▲▲△

EXTRA QUICK   NUT-FREE

PREP TIME: 5 minutes / **COOK TIME:** 10 minutes / **TOTAL TIME:** 15 minutes
MAKES: 1 sandwich

While living in Miami, I fell for their Cuban sandwiches. An authentic Cuban sandwich uses slow-cooked pork, but I use thinly sliced pork loin here for a tasty shortcut. It's topped with caramelized onions and Gouda cheese and pressed to perfection in a skillet.

3 tablespoons
   butter, divided

1 small onion, very
   thinly sliced

1 tablespoon apple
   cider vinegar

1 teaspoon dark
   brown sugar

1 hoagie roll

1 tablespoon
   English mustard

2 (4-ounce) slices
   peppered ham

8 ounces thinly sliced
   cooked pork loin

4 slices Gouda cheese

1 dill pickle, sliced into thin,
   long strips

1. In a small skillet over medium-low heat, combine 2 tablespoons of the butter with the onion, vinegar, and brown sugar. Simmer, stirring occasionally, for about 8 minutes, until the onion becomes translucent and then turns the color of caramel.

2. Slice the hoagie roll in half lengthwise and spread it with the mustard. On the bottom half of the hoagie, layer the ham, pork loin, cheese, and pickle strips. Top with the caramelized onion and cover with the other half of the roll.

3. In a small skillet over medium heat, melt the remaining 1 tablespoon butter. Once the butter begins to bubble, place the sandwich in the pan. Over the top of the sandwich, lay a piece of aluminum foil and press with a small cutting board for 30 seconds. Remove the foil and cutting board from the top of the sandwich and gently flip the sandwich over. Cover other side of sandwich with aluminum foil and press again with the small cutting board for 30 seconds. Remove the pressed sandwich from the pan and serve.

JAZZ IT UP: I like to add thin slices of green apple to the sandwich before pressing it.

Green Apple and Caramel Cheese Melt

▲ ▲ ▲

EXTRA QUICK   NUT-FREE   VEGETARIAN

PREP TIME: 10 minutes / **COOK TIME:** 15 minutes / **TOTAL TIME:** 25 minutes
SERVES: 1 to 2

This melt, served on a baguette, is a real treat. It's a great combination of sweet caramel offset by sharp cheddar and topped with tart green apple. You can also serve the caramel cheese sauce on the side with bite-size dipping pieces of crisp baguette and apple slices.

½ baguette

1½ tablespoons salted butter

1½ tablespoons all-purpose flour

⅓ cup Caramel Sauce (page 147)

2 cups grated extra-sharp cheddar cheese

1 Granny Smith apple, peeled, cored, and cut into ⅛-inch-thick slices

1. Set an oven rack 6 inches from the top heating element and preheat the oven to broil. Line a baking sheet with aluminum foil, shiny-side up.

2. Cut the baguette in half crosswise, and then in half lengthwise, so you have 4 pieces. Set the baguette on the prepared sheet and place it under the broiler for 2 minutes. Remove the baguette from the oven and let it cool, then use your fingers to scoop out the center of the bread. Set aside on the tray.

3. In a large skillet over medium-high heat, cook the butter for about 4 minutes, until it begins to bubble and turns golden in color. Reduce the heat to medium, whisk in the flour, and cook for 2 minutes; it will turn a light brown. Add the caramel and whisk for about 1 minute, until smooth. Reduce the heat to low, add the cheese, and cook for about 2 minutes, continuously stirring until the cheese melts and the sauce is thickened and creamy.

CONTINUED >

Green Apple and Caramel Cheese Melt CONTINUED

4. Spoon the cheese sauce into the channels in the baguette pieces. Top them with apple slices. Bake them under the broiler for 3 minutes, until browned and bubbling.

PRO TIP: You can use the toasted pieces you scooped out of the baguette as croutons in your next salad; just tear them into bite-size pieces.

Crepes

▲▲▲

PREP TIME: 5 minutes / **COOK TIME:** 16 minutes / **TOTAL TIME:** 20 minutes

MAKES: 4 crepes

Crepes can be tricky to make at first, but they're a truly impressive and versatile dish that's worth the effort. It may take a couple of crepes to figure it out, but practice makes perfect, so don't give up. The secret is a hot skillet and a confident flip. Serve them with a sweet, creamy filling and fresh fruit.

FOR THE FILLING

¼ cup cottage cheese

2 tablespoons sugar

¼ teaspoon vanilla extract

FOR THE CREPES

½ cup flour

1 egg

¼ cup milk

¼ cup water

⅛ teaspoon salt

1 tablespoon butter

TO MAKE THE FILLING

1. In a small bowl, combine the cottage cheese, sugar, and vanilla extract by hand or with an electric mixer.

TO MAKE THE CREPES

2. In a small mixing bowl, combine the flour, egg, milk, water, and salt. Beat the batter on low using an electric hand mixer, or whisk by hand.

3. Heat the butter in a small skillet over medium-high heat. Then, slowly pour ¼ cup of the crepe batter into the pan. Cook for 2 minutes and flip. Cook the other side for 2 minutes and remove from the pan. Immediately spread the crepes with 1 to 2 tablespoons of the filling mixture and roll up like a jelly roll.

> **PRO TIP:** Crepes come out best when cooked patiently. Don't disturb them until they're ready to flip.

stuffed Acorn squash

▲▲▲

DAIRY-FREE   GLUTEN-FREE   NUT-FREE   VEGAN

PREP TIME: 10 minutes / **COOK TIME:** 1 hour 5 minutes / **TOTAL TIME:** 1 hour 15 minutes
MAKES: 2 halves

Acorn squash is its own serving bowl in this recipe. Here, we will make a stuffing of quinoa and vegetables with dried fruit and apples, all seasoned with warm flavors. Then, we'll fill the squash and bake it until softened. It makes a self-contained meal you can be proud of.

1 cup quinoa

2 cups water

¾ cup diced onion

1 medium carrot, peeled and diced

1 stalk celery, chopped

¼ teaspoon salt

2 teaspoons extra-virgin olive oil, divided

¼ cup diced apple

1 tablespoon freshly squeezed lemon juice

¼ cup dried cranberries

¼ cup toasted pumpkin seeds

¼ teaspoon freshly grated nutmeg

¼ teaspoon cinnamon

⅛ teaspoon freshly ground black pepper

1 medium acorn squash, halved lengthwise and seeded

1. Preheat the oven to 350°F.

2. In a medium pot over medium heat, combine the quinoa and water. Simmer for about 15 minutes, until fluffy. Drain and set aside.

3. In a small skillet over medium heat, put the onion, carrot, celery, salt, and 1 teaspoon olive oil. Cover and cook for about 7 minutes, until the vegetables are softened and the onion is translucent.

4. In a small bowl, toss the apple with the lemon juice until coated.

5. In a medium mixing bowl, combine the drained quinoa and vegetables. Stir in the apples, cranberries, pumpkin seeds, nutmeg, cinnamon, and pepper. Mix until well combined.

6. Brush the skin of the squash with the remaining olive oil. Place the squash, cut-sides down, in a 13-by-9-inch baking dish and add ½ inch of boiling water. Bake in the preheated oven on the center rack for 20 minutes, or until the squash is soft. Remove the squash from the oven and let it cool.

7. When it is cool enough to handle, place the squash, cut-sides up, on a baking sheet lined with aluminum foil. Fill the squash halves with the stuffing mixture and bake for about 25 minutes, until the tip of a paring knife can easily pierce the squash.

HELPFUL HINT: You can also cut each half of the squash down the center once cooked and serve it as a side dish.

Fettuccini
Alfredo, page 99

CHAPTER FIVE

Cooking for a Group

(MEATLESS)

Pasta with Olive Oil, Garlic, and Romano Cheese

▲△△

EXTRA QUICK   NUT-FREE   VEGETARIAN

PREP TIME: 5 minutes / **COOK TIME:** 10 minutes / **TOTAL TIME:** 15 minutes
SERVES: 4

. . . .

Pasta with olive oil and garlic, known as *spaghetti aglio e olio* in Italian, is a light and flavorful meal. Adding Romano cheese elevates this traditional pasta dish. For those busy nights when you need something in a pinch, skip the fast food and make this easy, quick meal instead.

¾ cup extra-virgin olive oil

3 medium to large garlic cloves, finely chopped

1 (16-ounce) package spaghetti

1½ cups grated Romano cheese

½ teaspoon salt

¼ teaspoon freshly ground black pepper

1. Cook the pasta according to the package directions. Drain the pasta in a colander, and then transfer it to a large serving bowl.

2. Heat the olive oil in a medium skillet over medium heat. Add the garlic and cook for about 1 minute, just until it begins to turn golden and becomes fragrant. Pour the oil and garlic over the cooked pasta. Sprinkle it with the Romano cheese and toss. Season with salt and pepper.

JAZZ IT UP: Try adding sliced black olives when tossing for added briny saltiness or red pepper flakes when cooking the garlic for added spice.

Italian Vegetable Casserole

▲△△

GLUTEN-FREE | NUT-FREE | VEGETARIAN

PREP TIME: 10 minutes / **COOK TIME:** 55 minutes / **TOTAL TIME:** 1 hour 5 minutes
SERVES: 8

Fresh vegetables seasoned with Italian dressing make this casserole a dinner favorite. If you have any leftovers, try using them as a filling for an omelet, or add broth or tomato juice and serve it as a vegetable soup.

⅓ cup Italian dressing

1 large onion, chopped

1 small, unpeeled eggplant, cubed

1 medium zucchini, cubed

1 large red bell pepper, chopped

8 ounces sliced fresh mushrooms

1 (14.5-ounce) can Italian-style stewed tomatoes, drained and diced

⅓ cup shredded Parmesan cheese

1. Preheat the oven to 350°F.

2. Heat the Italian dressing in a large skillet over medium heat. Add the onion and cook for 5 minutes, or until tender. Add the eggplant and continue cooking, stirring often, for 5 minutes. Add the zucchini, bell pepper, and mushrooms and stir. Add the tomatoes and bring to a boil. Reduce the heat to low, cover, and simmer for 15 minutes, or until the vegetables are tender, stirring occasionally. Pour the mixture into a 13-by-9-inch baking dish and sprinkle it with Parmesan cheese.

3. Bake on the center rack in the preheated oven for 30 minutes, until bubbly.

JAZZ IT UP: Add one teaspoon of Italian seasoning to the vegetables before adding the tomatoes for even more flavor.

One-Pot Zucchini Mushroom Pasta

▲△△

EXTRA QUICK   NUT-FREE   VEGETARIAN

PREP TIME: 10 minutes / **COOK TIME:** 10 minutes / **TOTAL TIME:** 20 minutes
SERVES: 4 to 6

This delicious dish features fresh vegetables and a subtle cream sauce, and it only takes one pot and less than 20 minutes to make it to the table. It's perfect for busy nights when you don't have time to cook an intricate recipe or deal with the dishes afterward.

1 pound pasta

2 zucchinis, thinly sliced

1 pound cremini mushrooms, thinly sliced

⅔ cup peas

2 garlic cloves, minced

½ teaspoon dried thyme

4½ cups water

¼ cup heavy (whipping) cream

½ teaspoon salt

¼ teaspoon freshly ground black pepper

⅓ cup grated Parmesan cheese

1. In a large pot, combine the pasta, zucchini, mushrooms, peas, garlic, thyme, and water. Bring to a boil over medium-high heat. Reduce the heat to medium-low and simmer, uncovered, for 10 minutes, or until the noodles are al dente or done to your preference. Drain any excess water.

2. Stir in the cream, salt, pepper, and Parmesan. Serve.

SUB IN: For a fun twist, if you have a spiralizer, you can spiralize the zucchinis to make your own zucchini noodles. Then, you can use these "zoodles" instead of the pasta.

vegetable Lasagna

▲△△

PREP TIME: 15 minutes / **COOK TIME:** 20 minutes / **TOTAL TIME:** 35 minutes
SERVES: 8

. . . .

This simple meatless lasagna features spinach, carrots, and cheese filling nestled between noodles and topped with mozzarella.

2 (10-ounce) packages frozen chopped spinach, thawed

2 cups small-curd cottage cheese

1 egg, beaten

1 teaspoon minced garlic

2 teaspoons Italian seasoning

1½ cups vegetable broth

1 tablespoon cornstarch

¼ teaspoon salt

Dash freshly ground black pepper

⅛ teaspoon nutmeg

6 lasagna noodles, divided

3 cups shredded carrot, steamed

¼ cup chopped onion

½ cup shredded mozzarella cheese

1. Preheat the oven to 350°F. Grease a 12-by-8-by-2-inch baking dish.

2. In a medium mixing bowl, combine the chopped spinach, cottage cheese, egg, garlic, and Italian seasoning and mix until well blended.

3. In a medium saucepan over medium heat, combine the broth and cornstarch, stirring until thickened and smooth. Stir in the salt, pepper, and nutmeg. Remove the sauce from the heat.

4. Spread ½ cup of the sauce on the bottom of the prepared baking dish. Add 3 of the lasagna noodles, setting them side by side to form a layer across the baking dish. Top the layer of noodles with the spinach and cottage cheese mixture. Place the 3 remaining noodles in a side by side layer on top of the spinach and cheese mixture. Add the carrot and onion to the remaining sauce and pour it over the noodles.

5. Cover the prepared lasagna with aluminum foil and bake it in the preheated oven for 15 minutes, or until the sauce is bubbling. Remove the lasagna from the oven, sprinkle it with mozzarella cheese, and let it rest for 10 minutes.

SUB IN: Try replacing half of the small-curd cottage cheese with ricotta cheese (amounting to 1 cup of each).

Potato Cheese Soup

▲△△

NUT-FREE   VEGETARIAN

PREP TIME: 15 minutes / **COOK TIME:** 30 minutes / **TOTAL TIME:** 45 minutes
SERVES: 8

Chunks of tender potatoes, celery, and onion combine in a creamy, cheesy broth in this chowder-like soup. Try tossing in a cup of chopped kale when you add the broth for a new twist (and some extra greens).

2 tablespoons butter

4 cups diced potatoes

⅓ cup chopped celery

½ cup chopped onion

3 cups vegetable broth

2 cups milk

1½ teaspoons salt

¼ teaspoon freshly ground
   black pepper

⅛ teaspoon paprika

1 cup shredded
   cheddar cheese

¼ cup croutons

1. In a large saucepan over medium heat, melt the butter with the potatoes, celery, and onion. Cook for 8 minutes, or until the celery softens and the onion becomes translucent.

2. Add the broth, cover, and simmer for about 8 minutes, until the potatoes are tender. With a fork or wooden spoon, lightly mash the potatoes. Whisk in the milk, salt, pepper, and paprika. Bring the soup to a simmer and add the cheese, stirring until the cheese melts. Remove the soup from the heat, spoon it into bowls, and serve it garnished with croutons.

JAZZ IT UP: Add a quarter teaspoon of your favorite hot sauce to the broth for a little bit of kick.

Fettuccini Alfredo

▲△△

`EXTRA QUICK` `NUT-FREE` `VEGETARIAN`

PREP TIME: 5 minutes / **COOK TIME:** 25 minutes / **TOTAL TIME:** 30 minutes
SERVES: 4

. . . .

When you discover how easy it is to make alfredo sauce from scratch, you'll never want it from a jar again. The key to a smooth, creamy alfredo is to simmer the sauce and whisk it often. Garnish with freshly chopped parsley, if you like.

½ cup butter

½ teaspoon minced garlic

2 cups heavy (whipping) cream

¼ cup grated Parmesan cheese

½ teaspoon salt

¼ teaspoon freshly ground black pepper

1 pound fettuccini noodles

1. Heat the butter and garlic in a medium saucepan over low heat. Stir as the butter begins to melt until the garlic is fragrant, and then add the cream. Using a whisk, stir the cream for about 6 minutes, until the butter melts completely. Slowly bring the mixture to a simmer and cook for about 3 more minutes. Add the Parmesan and simmer, while whisking often, for 15 minutes. Add the salt and pepper.

2. While you are making the alfredo sauce, cook the fettuccini noodles according to the package directions. Pour the sauce over the noodles and serve warm.

JAZZ IT UP: Add one cup of cooked peas or one cup of sautéed mushrooms to the alfredo sauce.

pumpkin soup

▲△△

GLUTEN-FREE NUT-FREE VEGETARIAN

PREP TIME: 10 minutes / **COOK TIME:** 50 minutes / **TOTAL TIME:** 1 hour
SERVES: 4

This is a soup that reminds me of fall with its warm flavors. It can be served all year round but is especially good on a cool, crisp day. Try garnishing it with roasted pumpkin seeds and a dollop of sour cream.

1 tablespoon butter

1 cup chopped onion

1 (15-ounce) can 100% pure pureed pumpkin

3 cups vegetable broth

1 teaspoon dried thyme

1 teaspoon salt

2 small bay leaves

1 cup light cream

1. In a medium saucepan over medium heat, cook the butter and onion for about 7 minutes, until the onion is translucent. Stir in the pumpkin, broth, thyme, salt, and bay leaves. Bring the soup to a boil, then reduce the heat to low and simmer for 15 minutes.

2. Remove the soup from the heat and pull out the bay leaves. Cover the soup and allow it to cool for 15 minutes. Add the cream and return the soup to low heat, stirring often, until it reaches your desired serving temperature (be careful not to bring the soup to a boil after adding the cream).

JAZZ IT UP: Garnish this soup with a dollop of sour cream and sprouted pumpkin seeds.

Tomato Spinach Pie

▲△△

NUT-FREE   VEGETARIAN

PREP TIME: 10 minutes / **COOK TIME:** 40 minutes / **TOTAL TIME:** 50 minutes
SERVES: 8 to 10

This only requires a bottom pie crust, and I take the shortcut and use a frozen crust that already comes in a pie plate. You can follow my lead or buy a refrigerated pie crust and follow the package directions to unfold it onto your own pie plate. Once you have the crust ready, you simply add a delicious filling made from fresh ingredients, bake, and serve. It's really that easy.

1 unbaked pie crust

1½ cups shredded
   mozzarella
   cheese, divided

5 Roma or
   medium tomatoes

1 cup baby spinach leaves

1 teaspoon minced garlic

½ cup mayonnaise

¼ cup grated
   Parmesan cheese

⅛ teaspoon freshly ground
   black pepper

1. Bake the pie crust according to the package directions, then remove it from the oven and sprinkle immediately with ½ cup of the mozzarella.

2. Adjust the oven temperature to 375°F, if needed, after baking the crust. Cut the tomatoes into thick slices and rest them on a folded paper towel to absorb any excess juices. Add the tomatoes to the baked crust, arranging them on top of the cheese. Chop the spinach and add it to the tomatoes.

3. In a medium bowl, combine the garlic, the remaining cup of mozzarella, the mayonnaise, Parmesan, and pepper. Spoon the mixture over the spinach and spread it to cover the pie.

4. Bake in the preheated oven for 35 minutes, or until the top is golden and bubbly. Serve warm.

JAZZ IT UP: Finely chop one small onion and sauté it in one tablespoon of butter until softened. Add the sautéed onion to the top of the tomato slices before adding the cheese filling.

Pesto Pasta with Sun-Dried Tomatoes

▲△△

VEGETARIAN

PREP TIME: 5 minutes / **COOK TIME:** 15 minutes / **TOTAL TIME:** 20 minutes
SERVES: 4

The star of this vegetarian pasta dish is the fresh pesto. You can use half a cup of premade pesto if you prefer, but making homemade pesto is fun and incredibly simple with a blender.

1 pound spiral-shaped pasta

¼ cup pine nuts (or walnuts), plus more for garnish

½ cup extra-virgin olive oil

¼ cup shredded Parmesan cheese

2 cups fresh basil leaves, packed

1 tablespoon freshly squeezed lemon juice

½ teaspoon salt

Dash freshly ground black pepper

1 cup frozen green peas, thawed

1 cup finely chopped oil-packed sun-dried tomatoes

1. Cook the pasta according to the package directions. Drain it in a colander, and then transfer it to a large mixing bowl.

2. This step is optional, but it does add a depth of flavor to the pesto. In a small, dry (no oil) skillet over medium heat, cook the nuts for 3 minutes, shaking the pan frequently to turn the nuts. Remove from the heat and add the nuts to the blender.

3. To the blender with the nuts, add the olive oil and Parmesan and blend until the mixture is smooth. Add the basil and pulse a few more times to break it down. Add the lemon juice, salt, and pepper and pulse twice.

4. To the large mixing bowl with the pasta, fold in the peas and sun-dried tomatoes. Pour the pesto sauce over all and toss to coat. Garnish the dish with additional Parmesan or nuts.

Zucchini Lasagna Rollups

▲▲△

GLUTEN-FREE NUT-FREE VEGETARIAN

PREP TIME: 15 minutes / **COOK TIME:** 25 minutes / **TOTAL TIME:** 40 minutes
MAKES: 14 rollups

If you love lasagna, you'll love this vegetable version. To keep the rolls together, I find it easiest to soak 14 toothpicks in water, and then use one in each rollup to hold it in place. Just be sure to give your guests a heads up before they dig in.

2 tablespoons butter

⅓ cup chopped onion

3 tablespoons cornstarch

1 teaspoon salt

⅛ teaspoon freshly ground black pepper

⅛ teaspoon dried thyme

1 cup grated zucchini

1½ cups ricotta cheese

1½ cups milk

⅓ cup mayonnaise

7 lasagna noodles, cooked, drained, and halved lengthwise

2 tablespoons grated Parmesan cheese

1. Preheat the oven to 325°F.

2. Melt the butter in a large saucepan over medium heat. Add the onion and sauté for about 7 minutes, until tender and translucent.

3. In a small mixing bowl, combine the cornstarch, salt, pepper, and thyme and stir until well combined. Add the mixture to the sautéed onion and stir until it begins to thicken into a sauce. Stir in the zucchini.

4. In a separate small mixing bowl, combine ⅓ cup of the sauce with the ricotta and stir to combine. Place 2 tablespoons of the ricotta mixture on a noodle half and roll it up. Secure each rollup with a toothpick.

5. Pour half of the remaining sauce (without the ricotta) in the bottom of a 13-by-9-inch pan. Add the rollups. Once all of the rollups are in the pan, pour the rest of the remaining sauce over the top. Sprinkle with Parmesan and bake on the center rack in the preheated oven for 20 minutes, until the sauce bubbles.

PRO TIP: Spread the ricotta mixture on each noodle half in a thin and even layer to make rolling easier.

Tomato, Potato, and Leek Gratin

▲ ▲ ▲

GLUTEN-FREE   NUT-FREE   VEGETARIAN

PREP TIME: 15 minutes / **COOK TIME:** 1 hour / **TOTAL TIME:** 1 hour 15 minutes
SERVES: 8

This gratin is one of my family's favorite meals and creates a beautiful display of colors on the table when served. It's layered in thirds of thinly sliced potatoes, sautéed leeks, and chunks of tomatoes. In the oven, the gratin will thicken in its own juices, creating rustic flavors.

2 leeks

2 tablespoons butter

1¼ teaspoons salt, divided

5 medium potatoes

1½ tablespoons extra-virgin olive oil

½ teaspoon freshly ground black pepper

1 teaspoon fresh thyme, chopped

1 (28-ounce) can Italian-style plum tomatoes

½ cup packed fresh basil leaves, chopped

1¼ cups Parmesan cheese, divided

½ cup heavy (whipping) cream

1. Preheat the oven to 400°F.

2. Rinse the leeks under cold water, cut off the roots and the dark green part, and then slice the white part into ¼-inch-thick slices. Add these slices to a bowl of cold water and stir with your hands until all the dirt and sand is off. Then strain in a colander.

3. In a medium skillet over medium heat, melt the butter, then add the sliced leeks and cook for about 7 minutes, until the leeks are wilted and tender. Sprinkle them with ¼ teaspoon of the salt and remove them from the heat.

4. While the leeks sauté, cut the potatoes into ⅛-inch-thick slices. Place the slices in a medium bowl filled with cold water for 10 seconds, and then drain the water, leaving them in the bowl. Toss the slices with olive oil, ½ teaspoon salt, pepper, and thyme.

5. Place a colander in the sink and pour the can of tomatoes into it. Transfer the tomatoes to a cutting board and slice them into large chunks. Place the chunks in a small bowl and toss with the remaining ½ teaspoon salt, as well as the basil, 1 cup of the Parmesan, and the cream.

6. In an 8-by-8-inch baking dish, spread ⅓ of the leeks. Overlap ⅓ of the potato slices to cover the pan. Spread ⅓ of the tomatoes over the potatoes. Repeat layering two more times.

7. Place the gratin on the center rack in the preheated oven and bake for 35 minutes. The potatoes will begin to brown. Remove the casserole and sprinkle it with the remaining ¼ cup of Parmesan. Return it to the oven and cook for 25 minutes, until the surface is bubbling and the cheese is browned. Remove it from the oven and let rest for 5 minutes before serving.

HELPFUL HINT: Make sure you clean the leeks with great care, paying special attention to where the leek changes from green to white.

Ricotta Zucchini Meatballs

▲▲▲

EXTRA QUICK   NUT-FREE   VEGETARIAN

PREP TIME: 20 minutes / **COOK TIME:** 10 minutes / **TOTAL TIME:** 30 minutes
SERVES: 4

These delicious "meatballs" are actually meatless. They have an incredible texture and pack lots of flavor, making them a star dish served over pasta or zoodles (see Tip on page 96).

3 zucchinis

1 large onion

½ cup ricotta cheese

½ cup Parmesan cheese

1 cup panko breadcrumbs

1 egg

1 tablespoon
   Italian seasoning

2 teaspoons minced garlic

¼ cup fresh basil, chopped

5 tablespoons vegetable oil

2 cups tomato sauce

1. In a medium mixing bowl, using a box grater, grate the zucchinis and onion. Transfer the grated vegetables to a clean dishcloth or heavy-duty paper towel and squeeze the water out. Set aside.

2. In a medium mixing bowl, combine the ricotta, Parmesan, panko breadcrumbs, egg, Italian seasoning, garlic, and basil and stir until well combined. Add the grated zucchini mixture and mix until well combined.

3. In a small skillet over medium-low heat, begin heating the vegetable oil. Shape the zucchini mixture into 1- to 2-inch round "meatballs." Add the balls to the heated oil and cook for 5 minutes, continually moving the balls around to lightly brown all of the sides.

4. Place an oven rack in the top slot under the broiler and preheat the oven to broil. Transfer the meatballs to an 8-by-8-inch baking pan. Pour the tomato sauce over the balls and broil for 4 minutes. Remove them from the oven and serve immediately.

PRO TIP: A melon baller is a great tool to measure and shape the meatballs.

vegetarian Egg Rolls

▲▲▲

DAIRY-FREE NUT-FREE VEGETARIAN

PREP TIME: 15 minutes / **COOK TIME:** 30 minutes / **TOTAL TIME:** 45 minutes

MAKES: 30 egg rolls

These vegetarian egg rolls are quite tasty, but they take some patience and you may have to practice rolling them. Be sure to pay attention to safety since you will be frying these egg rolls in hot oil. Wear an apron and long oven mitts, make sure your hair is pulled back, and have your egg rolls all rolled and ready to go before you begin frying.

4 cups shredded cabbage

2½ cups fresh bean sprouts, chopped

1 cup shredded carrot

½ cup minced green onion

½ cup fresh spinach

½ cup chopped broccoli

½ cup chopped green bell pepper

½ cup sliced mushrooms

3 tablespoons vegetable oil, plus more for frying

1 (2-ounce) jar diced pimentos, drained

¼ cup soy sauce

2 tablespoons sugar

3 tablespoons cornstarch, divided

1. In a large mixing bowl, combine the cabbage, bean sprouts, carrot, green onion, spinach, broccoli, green bell pepper, and mushrooms and toss to mix well.

2. Heat 3 tablespoons of the vegetable oil in a preheated large skillet over medium-low heat for 1 minute, working the oil up the sides of the pan. Add the combined vegetables and pimento (you may have to work in batches depending on how large your skillet is). Cook the vegetables for 3 minutes, or until crisp-tender. Turn off the heat and set the vegetables aside.

3. In a small mixing bowl, combine the soy sauce, sugar, 2 tablespoons of the cornstarch, cayenne pepper, and garlic. Whisk until it's well mixed and the sugar is dissolved. Add the sauce to the vegetables and pimento, continually stirring for 1 minute.

CONTINUED >

. . . .

¼ teaspoon
   cayenne pepper

¼ teaspoon minced garlic

2 tablespoons water

1 (1-pound) package egg
   roll wrappers

4. Combine the remaining tablespoon of cornstarch and the water in a separate bowl and set aside.

5. To the center of each egg roll wrapper, add 1 heaping tablespoon of the vegetable filling. Fold the top edge of the wrapper over the filling, then fold the left and right sides over the filling. Lightly brush the exposed edge of the wrapper with the cornstarch mixture. Tightly roll the filled end of the wrapper toward the exposed edge, gently pressing to seal. Secure each egg roll with a toothpick.

6. Heat 2 inches of vegetable oil in a pan to 375°F. Place 2 egg rolls in the hot oil and fry them for 35 seconds on each side, or until golden brown. Drain them on paper towels and remove the toothpicks. Repeat with the remaining egg rolls.

> **PRO TIP:** Fill and roll in batches! Set out three or four egg roll wrappers at a time, add filling to each, and then roll and seal them. This can help keep things moving.

Stir Fry Zucchini Noodles

▲▲▲

DAIRY-FREE   GLUTEN-FREE   NUT-FREE   VEGAN

PREP TIME: 20 minutes / **COOK TIME:** 6 minutes / **TOTAL TIME:** 26 minutes
SERVES: 4

This delicious low-carb dish is a great way to enjoy zucchini. To replace the pasta, we will transform zucchini into noodles, also known as zoodles (see Tip on page 96). A spiralizer tool is the easiest tool for this recipe; however, you can also use a vegetable peeler and a chef's knife to make zoodles. You'll want to discard the seedy inner flesh as it can make the zoodles bitter. For another great meal option, try exchanging the teriyaki sauce for my Tomato Sauce (page 130) and serve the dish with my Ricotta Zucchini Meatballs (page 106).

4 zucchinis

2 tablespoons vegetable oil

2 yellow onions, cut into thin strips

2 tablespoons teriyaki sauce

1 tablespoon soy sauce

1 tablespoon sesame seeds

1. Use a spiralizer to turn all 4 zucchinis into zoodles. If you don't have a spiralizer, you can use a vegetable peeler to cut the zucchinis lengthwise into long strips. Once you have peeled all the flesh off the zucchinis, use a knife to cut skinny strips (the width you want your noodles). Place the zoodles on folded paper towels to absorb the moisture.

2. Heat the vegetable oil in a large skillet over medium heat. Add the onions and cook for about 4 minutes, until tender. Add the zoodles and cook for 2 minutes, until tender.

3. In a small bowl, combine the teriyaki sauce and soy sauce and whisk together. Stir in the sesame seeds, add the mixture to the zoodles and onions, and toss to coat.

> **PRO TIP:** Be careful not to overcook the zoodles. Cook them only until they're tender or else they can get mushy.

Chicken Enchiladas, page 133

CHAPTER SIX

Cooking for a Group

(MEAT AND SEAFOOD)

Easy Beef Stroganoff

▲△△

NUT-FREE

PREP TIME: 10 minutes / **COOK TIME:** 25 minutes / **TOTAL TIME:** 35 minutes
SERVES: 6

Stroganoff was one of my favorite dishes when I was growing up. Tender beef coated in a thick brown gravy over egg noodles is easy to make. It's sure to become one of your favorite dishes, too.

1 pound egg noodles

¼ cup butter

1 garlic clove, chopped

1 cup chopped onion

1 pound beef steak, cubed

2 cups button mushrooms, sliced

1 (10.5-ounce) can condensed beef broth

1 cup sour cream

2½ tablespoons flour

Pinch salt

Dash freshly ground black pepper

1. Prepare the noodles per the package directions.

2. In a large skillet over medium-high heat, melt the butter. Add the garlic and onion and cook for 7 minutes, or until the onion becomes translucent. Add the beef and reduce the heat to medium. Cover and cook for about 12 minutes, until the beef is tender. Remove the lid, add the mushrooms, and cook for 5 minutes, or until the mushrooms become wilted. Add the beef broth and bring it to a boil.

3. In a small mixing bowl, whisk together the sour cream and flour. Once the beef mixture is boiling, whisk the sour cream and flour mixture into the beef mixture and stir continuously until the sauce thickens. Add salt and pepper to taste. Serve over the prepared egg noodles.

SUB IN: You can use two cups of cooked rice in place of the egg noodles.

parmesan Chicken

▲△△

NUT-FREE

PREP TIME: 10 minutes / **COOK TIME:** 1 hour / **TOTAL TIME:** 1 hour 10 minutes
SERVES: 4

This savory recipe is a cinch to make and features tender chicken breasts baked in a Parmesan crust. It's delicious as is, served with a side of vegetables. You can also add a slice of mozzarella to the chicken during the last four minutes of baking and serve it over noodles, topped with my Tomato Sauce (page 130).

1 cup seasoned stuffing mix, crushed

⅔ cup grated Parmesan cheese

¼ cup dried parsley flakes

4 boneless, skinless chicken breasts

⅓ cup butter, melted

1. Preheat the oven to 350°F. Line a cookie sheet with aluminum foil.

2. In a medium bowl, mix together the stuffing mix, Parmesan, and parsley until well combined.

3. Dip each chicken breast in melted butter, then coat it with the stuffing mixture. Place the coated chicken on the prepared cookie sheet. Repeat with the remaining chicken breasts.

4. Bake the coated chicken on the center rack in the preheated oven for 1 hour, or until it's no longer pink in the center and an inserted meat thermometer reads 165°F.

PRO TIP: For even cooking, place each chicken breast in a resealable bag and roll it with a rolling pin until it is half an inch thick before coating.

Creamy Pork Chop Casserole

▲△△

NUT-FREE

PREP TIME: 10 minutes / **COOK TIME:** 55 minutes / **TOTAL TIME:** 1 hour 5 minutes
SERVES: 6

This casserole features golden pork chops baked in a creamy sauce with potatoes and cheese and topped with French fried onions. If there are any leftovers, they pair well with fried eggs.

1 tablespoon vegetable oil

6 (½- to ¾-inch-thick) pork chops

Pinch salt, plus ½ teaspoon

1 (10¾-ounce) can condensed cream of celery soup

½ cup milk

½ cup sour cream

¼ teaspoon freshly ground black pepper

1 (24-ounce) bag frozen hash brown potatoes, thawed

1 cup shredded cheddar cheese, divided

1 (2.8-ounce) can French fried onions, divided

1. Preheat the oven to 350°F.

2. Heat the vegetable oil in a large skillet over medium heat for 30 seconds. Add the pork chops and cook for 6 minutes, or until golden brown. Turn the pork chops over and cook for another 6 minutes, or until golden brown. Drain and discard the oil. Sprinkle the chops with salt and set aside.

3. In a large bowl, combine the soup, milk, sour cream, pepper, and the remaining ½ teaspoon of salt. Stir in the potatoes, ½ cup of the cheese, and ½ can of the French fried onions. Spoon the mixture into a 9-by-13-inch baking dish. Arrange the pork chops on top of the mixture.

4. Cover and bake the casserole on the center rack in the preheated oven for 35 minutes, or until the chops are done and the mixture is bubbly. Remove the cover and top the chops with the remaining ½ cup of cheese and half can of French fried onions. Return the casserole to the oven and bake uncovered for 5 more minutes, or until the onions are golden brown.

PRO TIP: Always use a meat thermometer to check the internal temperature of pork. It should read 145°F for pork chops.

Chicken and Rice Casserole

▲△△

NUT-FREE

PREP TIME: 10 minutes / **COOK TIME:** 1 hour 15 minutes /
TOTAL TIME: 1 hour 25 minutes
SERVES: 4

This casserole uses converted or parboiled rice. This rice takes a little longer to cook than regular white rice, which helps it stay firm but tender in a casserole. You can typically find this rice in the same aisle as bagged rice but in a box.

1 (10.5-ounce) can cream of mushroom soup

1¼ cups milk

¾ cup parboiled or converted uncooked rice

1 (4-ounce) can mushroom stems and pieces

1 (1.5-ounce) package dry onion soup mix, divided

4 boneless, skinless chicken breasts

1. Preheat the oven to 350°F.

2. Mix the mushroom soup with the milk; set aside and reserve ½ cup of the mixture. Mix the remaining soup mixture with the rice, mushrooms (including their liquid), and half of the onion soup mix. Pour the mixture into a 13-by-9-inch baking dish. Place the chicken breasts on top. Pour the reserved soup mixture over the chicken breasts and sprinkle the remaining half of the onion soup mix over the top. Cover the pan with aluminum foil.

3. Bake the covered casserole on the center rack in the preheated oven for 1 hour. Uncover and bake for 15 minutes more. The rice should be tender and fluff with a fork, and the chicken should have an internal temperature of 165°F.

JAZZ IT UP: Add one cup of broccoli florets to the soup mixture along with the rice, mushrooms, and soup mix.

Burger and Bean Bake

▲△△

DAIRY-FREE   GLUTEN-FREE   NUT-FREE

PREP TIME: 10 minutes / **COOK TIME:** 1 hour / **TOTAL TIME:** 1 hour 10 minutes
SERVES: 4

This bake features three kinds of beans combined with ground beef and baked together for a savory meal that's packed with protein. Similar to chili, it also makes an excellent topping for baked potatoes!

1 pound ground beef

½ pound bacon, cooked and crumbled

1 onion, chopped

½ cup ketchup

¾ cup brown sugar

1 tablespoon vinegar

1 tablespoon dry mustard

1 (15-ounce) can pork and beans

1 (15-ounce) can butter beans, drained

1 (15-ounce) can kidney beans, drained

1. Preheat the oven to 350°F.

2. In a medium skillet over medium heat, cook the ground beef, breaking it apart as it cooks with a spatula, for about 8 minutes, until browned. Drain.

3. Add the cooked beef along with the bacon, onion, ketchup, brown sugar, vinegar, mustard, pork and beans, butterbeans, and kidney beans to a 13-by-9-inch baking dish and stir until the mixture is well combined. Spread it out evenly in the baking dish and bake on the center rack in the preheated oven for 1 hour, or until bubbly.

JAZZ IT UP: Top this dish with one cup of shredded cheddar cheese immediately after removing it from the oven.

Meatloaf

▲△△

DAIRY-FREE NUT-FREE

PREP TIME: 10 minutes / **COOK TIME:** 1 hour 30 minutes /
TOTAL TIME: 1 hour 40 minutes
SERVES: 6 to 8

This classic dish is best served with mashed potatoes (or Pumpkin Mashed Potatoes, page 54) and green vegetables for dinner. Leftovers can be sliced into bread-thick slices and used as a sandwich filling. You can even cut the leftover meatloaf into one-inch cubes and serve it in place of meatballs in a marinara sauce over noodles.

2 pounds ground beef

2 cups bread cubes

1 cup water

2 large eggs

½ cup chopped onion

1 (1.5-ounce) package dry onion soup mix

½ teaspoon salt

¼ teaspoon freshly ground black pepper

1. Preheat the oven to 350°F.

2. In a large mixing bowl, combine the ground beef, bread cubes, water, eggs, onion, soup mix, salt, and pepper until well blended. Transfer the mixture to a loaf pan and bake in the preheated oven for 1½ hours, or until the internal temperature reads 155°F to 160°F. Drain the grease.

3. Place a plate over the loaf pan and invert the meatloaf onto the plate. Lift off the loaf pan. Let the meatloaf rest for 10 minutes, then slice and serve.

> **JAZZ IT UP:** Top the meatloaf with my Ooey-Gooey Sauce before cooking: In a small bowl, mix together five teaspoons of packed brown sugar, ⅔ cup ketchup, one tablespoon of dry mustard, and two teaspoons of Worcestershire Sauce. Stir until the brown sugar is dissolved. Pour the sauce over the top of the meatloaf before placing in the oven.

sausage and pasta soup

▲△△

DAIRY-FREE   NUT-FREE

PREP TIME: 10 minutes / **COOK TIME:** 1 hour 10 minutes /
TOTAL TIME: 1 hour 20 minutes
SERVES: 4 to 6

I first tried this recipe when a friend who loves to cook served it on a soup bar one night during a get-together. This soup made such an impression that I had to call the next day to get his recipe. It has a warm tomato flavor with chunks of vegetables and sausage.

2 tablespoons extra-virgin olive oil

1 small onion, finely chopped

1 celery rib, finely chopped

1 garlic clove, minced

5 cups chicken stock

1 cup canned crushed tomatoes in puree

1 teaspoon Italian seasoning

½ teaspoon salt

¼ teaspoon freshly ground black pepper

⅓ cup small pasta

1 pound Italian sausage links, cut into ¼-inch thick slices

1. Heat the olive oil in a large stockpot over medium heat. Add the onion and celery, cover, and cook for 8 to 10 minutes, or until the onion is translucent and the celery is tender. Stir in the garlic and cook for about 30 seconds, just until fragrant.

2. Add the chicken stock, crushed tomatoes, Italian seasoning, salt, and pepper. Bring the soup to a simmer and reduce the heat to low, then add the pasta. Cook at a gentle simmer for about 10 minutes, until the pasta is almost done. Add the sausage and simmer for 30 to 50 minutes more.

JAZZ IT UP: Garnish this dish with fresh basil leaves.

Ham, Green Bean, and Potato Bake

▲△△

DAIRY-FREE   GLUTEN-FREE   NUT-FREE

PREP TIME: 5 minutes / **COOK TIME:** 50 minutes / **TOTAL TIME:** 55 minutes
SERVES: 4

This complete meal comes together in one dish and is incredibly easy to make. Feel free to add bell peppers or drained diced tomatoes to make this a beautiful dish full of color and flavor.

½ pound ham, cut into ½-inch pieces

3 medium white potatoes, peeled and cut into ½-inch cubes

1 (15-ounce) can cut green beans, drained

1 small onion, cut into ¼-inch dice

½ cup bottled Italian dressing

½ teaspoon salt

¼ teaspoon freshly ground black pepper

1. Preheat the oven to 350°F.

2. In an 8-by-8-inch baking dish, combine the ham, potatoes, green beans, onion, Italian dressing, salt, and pepper and stir until all is coated with the dressing. Cover the dish with aluminum foil and bake on the center rack in the preheated oven for 35 minutes. Uncover the dish and continue baking for another 15 minutes, or until the potatoes are tender when stabbed with a fork.

SUB IN: Use sliced kielbasa in place of the ham.

Creamy Chicken and Broccoli Casserole

▲△△

NUT-FREE

PREP TIME: 5 minutes / **COOK TIME:** 45 minutes / **TOTAL TIME:** 50 minutes
SERVES: 6

A long time ago, my friend made this casserole for my family, and we absolutely loved it. We moved a couple of times, and the recipe was lost. This is my version of my friend's lost casserole recipe. It's not entirely hers, but it's still a meal my family loves to see on the dinner table.

6 chicken breasts

1 quart chicken broth

1 (10.75-ounce) can cream of celery soup

1 (10.75-ounce) can cream of chicken soup

1 (8-ounce) package herb-seasoned breadcrumbs, divided

½ cup butter, melted

1 (12-ounce) bag frozen broccoli florets, thawed and drained

1. In a large saucepan over high heat, combine the chicken breasts and chicken broth, and then add enough water to bring the liquid ½ inch above the chicken. Reduce the heat to low as the liquid begins to boil, and simmer for 15 minutes, or until the internal temperature of the chicken is at least 165°F. Transfer the chicken to a plate and let it rest for 5 minutes, then chop into 1-inch cubes. Reserve the broth.

2. Preheat the oven to 350°F. Grease a 13-by-9-inch baking dish.

3. In a medium mixing bowl, combine the cream of celery and cream of chicken soups and 2 cups of the reserved broth and whisk until smooth.

4. In a small mixing bowl, combine ¾ cup of the bread-crumbs and the butter. Stir until the breadcrumbs are uniformly moist. Spread the breadcrumbs along the bottom of the prepared baking dish. Top them with the chicken chunks and broccoli florets. Pour the soup mixture over the chicken and broccoli and sprinkle the mixture with the remaining (dry) breadcrumbs.

5. Bake uncovered on the center rack in the preheated oven for 45 minutes, or until bubbly.

SUB IN: Try using Italian seasoned panko breadcrumbs instead of herb-seasoned breadcrumbs.

stuffed pepper soup

▲△△

DAIRY-FREE NUT-FREE

PREP TIME: 15 minutes / **COOK TIME:** 30 minutes / **TOTAL TIME:** 45 minutes
SERVES: 6

Imagine stuffed bell peppers deconstructed and in soup form. This soup offers the flavors of that classic dish in every spoonful. If you want a thicker soup, just cook it longer. You can also make it ahead of time and place it in the refrigerator after adding the rice, and it will thicken there as well. I like it served with rolls and garnished with sour cream.

1 medium onion, chopped

1 pound ground chuck

2 bell peppers (any color), seeded and chopped

4 tablespoons ketchup

3 (10.75-ounce) cans condensed tomato soup

4 cups water

1 (10.75-ounce) can beef broth

2 cups cooked rice

1. In a large skillet over medium heat, combine the onion and ground meat. Cook for about 10 minutes, breaking the meat apart with a spatula as it cooks, until the onion is translucent and the meat has browned. Drain.

2. In a large saucepan over medium-high heat, combine the meat mixture with the bell peppers, ketchup, tomato soup, water, and beef broth. Stir to combine and bring the soup to a boil, then reduce the heat to medium and simmer until the soup reaches your desired consistency. Add the rice 5 minutes before serving.

JAZZ IT UP: Serve this soup topped with shredded cheddar cheese.

Quick-Seared Hamburgers

▲△△

EXTRA QUICK   GLUTEN-FREE   NUT-FREE

PREP TIME: 10 minutes / **COOK TIME:** 20 minutes / **TOTAL TIME:** 30 minutes
SERVES: 4 to 6

These quick-seared hamburgers are so easy to make and taste delicious. A touch of butter adds great flavor. This recipe sticks to the basics, but you can also add chopped onions or grated cheese, or try using steak seasoning in place of the salt and pepper, to make these burgers to your liking. Adjust the cooking time if you prefer a more well-done burger.

1½ pounds ground chuck or ground round

1 teaspoon butter, softened, plus more for spreading

1 teaspoon vegetable oil

½ teaspoon salt

¼ teaspoon freshly ground black pepper

1. Shape the meat into 6 (⅛-inch-thick) patties.

2. Heat the butter and oil in a large skillet over medium-high heat for about 1 minute, until it begins to smoke. Quickly add the burgers and brown them, one side at a time, for about 2½ minutes. Flip the burgers and brown their other sides for about 2½ minutes.

3. Transfer the cooked patties to a plate and spread each burger with the softened butter, then sprinkle them with the salt and pepper.

JAZZ IT UP: Serve these burgers with hamburger buns and top them with all your favorite burger ingredients.

Herbed Turkey Meatballs

▲ △ △

EXTRA QUICK   NUT-FREE

PREP TIME: 5 minutes / **COOK TIME:** 20 minutes / **TOTAL TIME:** 25 minutes
MAKES: 30 meatballs

These are the only meatballs my family will eat. They are a blend of ground turkey and spices, rolled into meatballs and baked in the oven. They pair well with pasta and marinara or nestled in a submarine roll. I make them ahead of time and store them in a resealable freezer bag to keep on hand for an easy addition to pasta dishes.

¼ cup breadcrumbs

1½ teaspoons dried basil

1 teaspoon garlic powder

½ teaspoon oregano

½ teaspoon salt

¼ teaspoon freshly ground black pepper

1 pound ground turkey

1 egg, lightly beaten

1. Preheat the oven to 400°F. Cover a 15-by-10-by-1-inch baking pan with aluminum foil.

2. In a large bowl, mix the breadcrumbs, basil, garlic powder, oregano, salt, and pepper. Add the ground turkey and egg, then mix well. Form the mixture into 1-inch meatballs and place them on the prepared baking pan.

3. Bake for 15 to 20 minutes, or until cooked through. Drain well.

PRO TIP: These meatballs freeze well. Place them in a freezer-safe container and store them for up to 30 days.

Fried Chicken in Mushroom Sauce

▲ ▲ △

NUT-FREE

PREP TIME: 5 minutes / **COOK TIME:** 1 hour 10 minutes / **TOTAL TIME:** 1 hour 15 minutes
SERVES: 4

For this recipe, you'll first fry the chicken, and then bake it in a creamy mushroom sauce. You can add sliced, sautéed mushrooms to the sauce before pouring it over the chicken if you want. I love this dish served with mashed potatoes or rice.

1 (2½-pound) fryer chicken, cut up

½ teaspoon salt

¼ teaspoon freshly ground black pepper

4 tablespoons vegetable oil

1 (10.5-ounce) can condensed cream of mushroom soup

1½ cups water

½ cup diced celery

¼ cup diced green bell pepper

1. Preheat the oven to 425°F.

2. Sprinkle the chicken with the salt and pepper. Heat the vegetable oil in a large skillet over medium-high heat for 1 minute. Add the chicken and cook for 5 minutes, or until golden brown, and then turn over the chicken pieces and cook the other side for 5 minutes, or until golden brown. Remove the skillet from the heat and transfer the chicken to a 13-by-9-inch baking pan.

3. In a medium mixing bowl, combine the mushroom soup with the water and stir to a smooth consistency. Pour the mixture over the chicken pieces in the baking pan. Sprinkle them with the celery and green bell pepper.

4. Bake on the center rack of the preheated oven, uncovered, occasionally basting with the gravy in the pan, for 1 hour, or until the chicken is tender and reads 165°F on a meat thermometer.

JAZZ IT UP: Add half a teaspoon of paprika to the soup mixture.

Chili Con Carne

▲ ▲ △

DAIRY-FREE   EXTRA QUICK   GLUTEN-FREE   NUT-FREE

PREP TIME: 10 minutes / **COOK TIME:** 1 hour 40 minutes /
TOTAL TIME: 1 hour 50 minutes

SERVES: 6

. . . .

Chili con carne means chili with meat in Spanish. I add beans to my chili at the end, but some people feel beans don't belong in chili, so I'll leave that up to you. This chili recipe is somewhat mild, but if you like more heat, add more chili powder to your taste.

3 tablespoons vegetable oil

1 cup thinly sliced onion

4 tablespoons diced green
   bell pepper

2 pounds rump roast, cut
   in to ½-inch cubes

3 tablespoons chili powder

¼ cup cold water

1 cup boiling water

1 cup canned tomato juice

½ teaspoon salt

2 teaspoons
   granulated sugar

3 garlic cloves, minced

2 (15-ounce) cans red
   kidney beans (optional)

1. Heat the vegetable oil in a large skillet over medium-high heat for 1 minute. Add the onion and green bell pepper and cook for 7 minutes, or until the bell peppers are tender and the onion is translucent. Add the beef and cook, uncovered, for about 8 minutes, until it begins to sizzle and brown.

2. In a small mixing bowl, combine the chili powder with the cold water and whisk to create a smooth paste. Set aside.

3. Add the boiling water and tomato juice to the beef mixture in the skillet, whisk in the chili powder/water paste until blended, and then add the salt, sugar, and minced garlic.

4. Cover the skillet, reduce the heat to medium-low, and simmer for 1 hour. Remove the cover and simmer for 30 minutes more, or until the meat is tender. Add 1 or 2 tablespoons of hot water if the mixture thickens before the meat is tender. Add the kidney beans (if using) and heat for 5 minutes.

Roasted Turkey

▲▲△

DAIRY-FREE   GLUTEN-FREE   NUT-FREE

PREP TIME: 5 minutes / **COOK TIME:** 3 hours / **TOTAL TIME:** 3 hours 5 minutes

SERVES: 10 to 12

. . . .

It's easier than you think to prepare a roasted turkey with pan gravy and home-made cranberry sauce (see pages 128 and 129 that follow). Gather your family and friends and amaze them with a made-from-scratch Thanksgiving feast any day of the year!

1 (14-pound) whole turkey

1 tablespoon salt

1. Preheat the oven to 450°F.

2. In a deep roasting pan, place the turkey, breast-side up. Sprinkle with salt and roast in the preheated oven for 1 hour. Using a spoon or baster, baste the turkey with the juices in the bottom of the pan, and then decrease the oven temperature to 350°F. Roast the turkey for 2 hours more, or until the turkey is golden brown and cooked through. The temperature measured on a meat thermometer from the thigh should read 165°F.

3. Transfer the turkey to a platter and pour the juices into a medium mixing bowl. Be sure to scrape the particles stuck to the bottom of the pan into the liquid.

PRO TIP: Baking the turkey breast-side up will ensure that the white meat is moist and juicy.

Pan Gravy

▲▲△

PREP TIME: 5 minutes / **COOK TIME:** 10 minutes / **TOTAL TIME:** 15 minutes
SERVES: 4 to 6

The drippings from your roasted turkey (page 127) contain all the flavor you'll need to make homemade gravy. You'll make a slurry with flour and water to thicken the juices and transform them into a golden pan gravy.

1 cup all-purpose flour

1 cup water

Pan drippings from the turkey

Salt

Freshly ground black pepper

1. In a small mixing bowl, whisk the flour and water together until smooth.

2. In a large saucepan over high heat, bring the turkey drippings (juices) to a slow boil for about 4 minutes.

3. Slowly add the flour mixture, whisking continuously, until the gravy is your desired consistency and a golden color. Taste the gravy, add salt or pepper as necessary, and serve.

PRO TIP: Make sure to scrape all the "stuff" stuck to the roasting pan into your gravy. This is where the flavor is!

Fresh Cranberry Sauce

▲▲△

DAIRY-FREE   GLUTEN-FREE   NUT-FREE   VEGAN

PREP TIME: 5 minutes / **COOK TIME:** 15 minutes / **TOTAL TIME:** 20 minutes
MAKES: 3 cups

My kids love to make fresh cranberry sauce. As the juice and liquid heat up, you can hear the cranberries burst. It also fills the kitchen with an incredible aroma.

1 (12-ounce) bag cranberries, rinsed and drained

½ cup freshly squeezed orange juice

1 orange, peeled, segmented, and chopped

1 cup sugar

1 teaspoon freshly squeezed lemon juice

1. In a large saucepan over medium heat, combine the cranberries, orange juice, chopped orange, sugar, and lemon juice and bring to a boil, continually stirring, for about 5 minutes, until the sugar dissolves.

2. Reduce the heat to medium-low and simmer while constantly stirring for 10 minutes, or until the sauce is your desired thickness.

JAZZ IT UP: Stir ¼ cup of chopped walnuts into the finished sauce.

Tomato Sauce

▲▲△

DAIRY-FREE   GLUTEN-FREE   NUT-FREE

PREP TIME: 10 minutes / **COOK TIME:** 3 hours / **TOTAL TIME:** 3 hours 10 minutes
SERVES: 12

This classic tomato sauce is my family's favorite because it goes with everything. We eat it over noodles, chicken, and pork chops and as spaghetti sauce, lasagna sauce, and pizza sauce; some of my kids even put it in a bowl and eat it like soup! It's definitely worth the effort. I usually make this recipe and freeze what we don't use in gallon-size resealable bags.

1 pound sweet Italian sausage

2 pork chops (with bone)

2 garlic cloves, finely chopped

4 (28-ounce) cans peeled Italian tomatoes or crushed tomatoes

2 fresh basil leaves

7 cups water

3 tablespoons dried parsley

¼ teaspoon Italian seasoning

½ teaspoon salt

¼ teaspoon freshly ground black pepper

5 (6-ounce) cans tomato paste

1. In a large saucepot over medium heat, cook the sausage and pork chops for about 8 minutes, until brown. Add the garlic and stir for about 30 seconds, until fragrant.

2. Add the tomatoes, one can at a time, to a blender with the basil and puree.

3. Next, add the water, parsley, Italian seasoning, salt, and pepper to the pot you cooked the meat in. Then add the pureed tomatoes and stir in the tomato paste, bring the sauce to a slow boil, and then reduce the heat to low. Simmer for 3 hours (you may need a splash guard, but do not cover the sauce), stirring every 10 minutes.

PRO TIP: Make this sauce, and then freeze the leftovers in one-cup portions. You can then pull out and reheat the sauce for dipping bread sticks, making pasta or lasagna, or using as a pizza sauce.

Chicken Vegetable Soup

▲▲△

DAIRY-FREE   GLUTEN-FREE   NUT-FREE

PREP TIME: 15 minutes / **COOK TIME:** 2 hours / **TOTAL TIME:** 2 hours 15 minutes
SERVES: 10

This Chicken Vegetable Soup adds potatoes, celery, onions, carrots, and chicken to broth for a warm cup of soup. Make a batch for a comforting meal or when you have a cold. It's a great remedy!

2 quarts water

3 pounds skinned chicken pieces

1 large onion, cut in to quarters

2 bay leaves

2 cups chopped carrot

1 cup chopped celery

2 cups cubed potatoes

¼ cup fresh parsley leaves

1 (10.75-ounce) can chicken broth

½ teaspoon salt

½ teaspoon freshly ground black pepper

1 teaspoon butter (optional)

1. In a large pot, combine the water, chicken pieces, onion, and bay leaves. Bring to a boil over medium-high heat, reduce the heat to medium, and simmer covered for 1½ hours, or until the chicken is tender. Remove the chicken and cut the meat off the bones when cooled. Cut the chicken meat into cubes. Discard the bones and bay leaves. Skim and discard the fat.

2. Add the carrot, celery, and potatoes to the boiled chicken broth. Over medium-high heat, bring the pot to a boil and cook for about 15 minutes, until the vegetables are tender. Add the cubed chicken, parsley, canned broth, salt, and pepper. Reduce the heat to medium-low and simmer for 15 minutes to combine the flavors. Add the butter just before serving, if desired.

> **JAZZ IT UP:** Bring the soup to a boil, add one 16-ounce package of egg noodles to the soup, and simmer it for about nine minutes, until the noodles are tender.

Italian Roast Beef

▲▲△

DAIRY-FREE   GLUTEN-FREE   NUT-FREE

PREP TIME: 10 minutes / **COOK TIME:** 4 hours / **TOTAL TIME:** 4 hours 10 minutes
SERVES: 6 to 8

In this classic recipe, I'll show you how to season and cook a roast. You're also welcome to add more vegetables to the pan before roasting to create a complete meal. Try adding one potato (quartered) and two carrots (peeled) per guest.

1 (4-pound) boneless chuck roast

2 cups chopped celery

2 cups chopped onion

1 teaspoon salt

½ teaspoon freshly ground black pepper

2 to 3 cups water

1 (7-ounce) bottle ketchup

1 (12-ounce) bottle chili sauce

¼ cup vinegar

4 tablespoons Worcestershire sauce

2 tablespoons garlic powder

1 tablespoon chili powder

1 tablespoon Italian seasoning

1 tablespoon cornstarch (optional)

1. Preheat the oven to 250°F.

2. Place the chuck roast in a roasting pan. Add the celery and onion, and then sprinkle all with the salt and pepper.

3. In a large bowl, mix the water, ketchup, chili sauce, vinegar, Worcestershire sauce, garlic powder, chili powder, and Italian seasoning and pour the mixture over the beef. Cover the roast with aluminum foil and cook in the preheated oven for about 4 to 5 hours, or until the beef begins to separate easily.

4. Transfer the beef to a platter. Skim and discard the fat from the cooking broth with a spoon or baster. Separate the beef with a fork if desired.

5. In a small mixing bowl, combine 3 tablespoons of the beef juices and the cornstarch (if using). Whisk until smooth to make a slurry.

6. Put 2 cups of the beef juices into a large saucepan over medium heat, and whisk in the cornstarch slurry. Whisk constantly until the juices thicken to your desired gravy consistency.

PRO TIP: If this beef is prepared a day in advance, it is far easier to remove the fat from the broth when chilled.

Chicken Enchiladas

▲▲△

PREP TIME: 10 minutes / **COOK TIME:** 40 minutes / **TOTAL TIME:** 50 minutes
SERVES: 4

These filling enchiladas are stuffed with cheese and chicken. You can use two cups of leftover chicken to reduce the cooking time. Try serving them topped with sour cream, guacamole, black olives, sliced jalapeños, or your other favorite toppings.

2 cups water

1 cup long grain white rice, rinsed

2 tablespoons extra-virgin olive oil

2 chicken breasts

½ cup mayonnaise

1 teaspoon cumin

¼ teaspoon cayenne pepper, plus more for garnish

6 (6-inch) flour tortillas

1 (12-ounce) jar chunky salsa

1 cup shredded Monterey Jack cheese

1 tablespoon chopped cilantro (optional)

1. Preheat the oven to 350°F.

2. In a medium saucepan over medium heat, bring the water to a boil. Add the rice, stir, and bring back to a boil. Reduce the heat to medium-low and cover. Cook for about 12 minutes, until soft, and then fluff the rice with fork.

3. Heat the olive oil in a medium skillet over medium-high heat for 30 seconds, then add the chicken breasts and cook for 4 minutes. Turn the chicken breasts over and cook for another 4 minutes, or until the chicken is done—meaning it's no longer pink inside and an inserted meat thermometer reads 165°F. Transfer the chicken to a clean plate. Let it rest for 3 minutes before chopping it into cubes.

4. In a medium mixing bowl, mix the mayonnaise, cumin, and cayenne pepper together. Add the chicken and mix thoroughly to coat. Spoon ⅙ of the mixture onto each tortilla and roll it up. Place each roll, seam-side down, in a 12-by-18-inch baking dish. Pour the salsa over the tortilla rolls and sprinkle the cheese over the top of them.

CONTINUED >

5. Bake on the center rack in the preheated oven for 30 minutes, or until the sauce is bubbling and the cheese has melted.

6. Serve the enchiladas over the hot rice and garnish them with chopped cilantro (if using) and additional cayenne pepper if desired.

HELPFUL HINT: For mild enchiladas, omit the cayenne pepper. You can also prepare the rice in a rice cooker if you like.

Sherri's Split Pea Soup

▲ ▲ △

GLUTEN-FREE NUT-FREE

PREP TIME: 15 minutes / **COOK TIME:** 55 minutes / **TOTAL TIME:** 1 hour 10 minutes
SERVES: 6

This easy to prepare soup from my friend, Sherri, was always a family favorite. You can serve it as a main dish alongside a loaf of French bread or sourdough or as a comforting side dish. It's flexible and can be prepared with or without the meat, so feel free to adjust the recipe to make it a vegetarian dish.

1 (13-ounce) package dried split peas

1 tablespoon butter

3 medium carrots, peeled and chopped

3 celery stalks, chopped

1 medium onion, peeled and chopped

1 smoked sausage (such as kielbasa) or 1 meaty ham bone

7 cups water

½ teaspoon salt

½ teaspoon freshly ground black pepper

1. Sort through the dried split peas and remove any stones, mud, or debris. It's easiest to spread the peas on a lipped cooking sheet or clean, lightly colored towel. When done, add the peas to a bowl and rinse well in cold, running water. Drain and set aside.

2. In a large, covered stockpot over medium-high heat, melt the butter. Add the carrots, celery, and onion and sauté, stirring frequently, for about 7 minutes, until the onions are softened and starting to become translucent. Add the sausage or ham bone. Sauté for an additional 5 minutes to heat the meat. Add the split peas, water, salt, and pepper. Stir the contents to mix thoroughly. Bring the mixture to a boil, reduce the heat to low, and cover, leaving a small opening for venting. Cook for about 30 minutes, stirring every 10 minutes to keep the peas from clumping and sticking to the pot. Taste the vegetables, checking for flavor and tenderness. You may need to add more salt, if necessary. If the vegetables are not tender enough, continue cooking for an additional 10 minutes, until tender.

CONTINUED >

3. If using a meaty ham bone, use a slotted spoon to remove the ham bone. Pick the meat off the bone and return the meat to the soup. Discard the bone after removing the meat. If using sausage, remove it from the soup and place it on a plate.

4. Using an immersion blender in an up and down motion, blend the soup until it is nearly smooth. You can also use a spoon to mash the peas against the edge of the pot and stir them back in until the soup has reached your desired thickness (the spoon mashing technique will not yield a smooth soup). Add the meat back into the soup and stir to incorporate. Serve.

SUB IN: For a richer soup, substitute chicken broth for the water.

Potluck Lasagna

▲▲△

NUT-FREE

PREP TIME: 15 minutes / **COOK TIME:** 1 hour / **TOTAL TIME:** 1 hour 15 minutes
SERVES: 8 to 10

This lasagna comes together without much effort and can feed a crowd of eight to 10 people, making it a perfect potluck dish. It's a delicious take on the classic lasagna with the addition of ham, chicken, and broccoli.

12 lasagna noodles

6 ounces cooked ham, sliced

1 large onion, chopped

12 ounces fresh mushrooms, sliced

¼ cup butter

6 tablespoons flour

1 (10.5-ounce) can chicken broth

1⅔ cups milk

⅔ cup grated Parmesan cheese

¼ teaspoon freshly ground black pepper

⅛ teaspoon ground nutmeg

16 ounces frozen broccoli, thawed

1 cup shredded Gruyère or Swiss cheese, divided

2 cups cooked chicken or turkey, chopped

1. Preheat the oven to 350°F. Cook the lasagna noodles per the package directions, drain, and set aside. Cut one slice of the cooked ham into julienne strips and set aside.

2. In a large skillet over medium heat, sauté the onion and mushrooms in butter for about 7 minutes, until soft. Whisk in the flour and gradually whisk in the broth and milk until smooth. Add the Parmesan, pepper, and nutmeg. Bring the mixture to a boil and cook until the sauce is thickened, approximately 5 minutes. Then, stir in the broccoli.

3. Arrange 4 of the noodles in a 13-by-9-inch pan, overlapping them slightly. Spoon ⅓ of the broccoli mixture onto the noodles. Top it with ham, then sprinkle it with 1 cup of the cheese. Place 4 noodles on top of the cheese. Top with ⅓ broccoli mixture, then the chicken and ½ cup of the Gruyère. Top with the remaining noodles, laying them diagonally if desired. Spoon the remaining broccoli mixture over the noodles and top with the ham strips. Loosely cover the lasagna with aluminum foil.

4. Bake on the center rack in the preheated oven, covered, for about 35 minutes, until heated through. Sprinkle the lasagna with the remaining ½ cup of Gruyère. Remove the pan from the oven and let it stand for 10 minutes before serving.

Fish in Parchment Paper

▲▲▲

DAIRY-FREE   GLUTEN-FREE   NUT-FREE

PREP TIME: 1 hour / **COOK TIME:** 20 minutes / **TOTAL TIME:** 1 hour 20 minutes

SERVES: 4

In this fun recipe, you'll cook fish and vegetables in individual "envelopes" of parchment paper, making a unique serving (and one less pan to wash up!). For best results, do not marinate the fish for longer than two hours.

4 filets mild white fish (such as cod, tilapia, sole, or turbot)

½ cup mild extra-virgin olive oil, divided

1 teaspoon lemon pepper (optional)

1 medium eggplant

1 medium zucchini

1 medium summer squash

1 lemon

8 cooked shrimp (optional)

2 cups grape tomatoes

1. Place the fish in a zip-top plastic bag with 1 tablespoon of the olive oil and the lemon pepper, if using, to lightly coat the fish. Place the sealed bag in the refrigerator for 1 hour to marinate.

2. Preheat the oven to 350°F.

3. Cut the eggplant, zucchini, squash, and lemon into round slices.

4. Roll out parchment paper on a flat surface. Remove the fish from the refrigerator and place one fillet on the paper. Cut the paper so that there is a 4- to 6-inch margin of paper around each side of the fish. Place 1 to 2 slices of eggplant underneath the fish. On top of the fish, place 1 to 2 slices of lemon. Place 2 of the shrimp, if using, on top of the lemon and fish. Top with 3 to 4 grape tomatoes. Add ¼ of the zucchini and squash all around the sides of the fish so that the vegetables are on their sides leaning against the fish. Sprinkle with the remaining olive oil. Fold the paper around the fish like a present and wrap it with butchers' twine to secure the paper. Repeat for each fillet.

5. Place the wrapped fish filets on the center oven rack, with a baking sheet on the rack below to catch any juices, and bake in the preheated oven for 20 minutes, or until the fish flakes easily with a fork. Thicker filets may require additional cooking time.

6. Place a wrapped fish on each guest's plate and cut the parchment open. Serve in the juices inside the parchment paper.

JAZZ IT UP: Sprinkle the fish with 1 tablespoon of seafood seasoning after using the olive oil.

Hungarian Goulash

▲▲▲

PREP TIME: 10 minutes / **COOK TIME:** 2 hours 10 minutes /
TOTAL TIME: 2 hours 20 minutes
SERVES: 4 to 6

This hearty stew originated in medieval Hungary and is still an excellent comfort food. The scents of cayenne pepper and paprika in this traditional dish take me back to watching my grandmother cook.

4 tablespoons vegetable oil

1 garlic clove, minced

1 pound chuck roast, cut into 1-inch cubes

1 pound lean pork shoulder, cut into 1-inch cubes

1 (28-ounce) can diced tomatoes

2 bay leaves

¼ teaspoons of salt and freshly ground black pepper

⅛ teaspoon cayenne pepper

1 teaspoon paprika

12 pearl onions, peeled

6 medium potatoes, peeled and quartered

2 cups celery, cut into 2-by-1-inch strips

2 tablespoons flour

3 tablespoons water

1. Heat the vegetable oil in a deep saucepan over medium-high heat for 1 minute, and then add the garlic, stirring for about 30 seconds, just until fragrant. Add the chuck roast and pork shoulder and brown for about 8 minutes. Add the tomatoes, bay leaves, salt, pepper, cayenne pepper, and paprika, and stir until well combined. Cover the pot and simmer for 1 hour to let the flavors to blend. Add the onions, cover, and simmer for 30 minutes, until the onions are softened. Add the potatoes and celery and stir. Cover and continue cooking for an additional 30 minutes, or until the potatoes and celery are tender.

2. In a small mixing bowl, whisk the flour into the water until you have a smooth slurry. Remove the bay leaves and then slowly whisk the slurry into the goulash mixture, continually stirring until thoroughly combined. Continue to stir until the sauce thickens. Serve.

JAZZ IT UP: Serve this dish topped with a dollop of sour cream and garnished with thinly sliced green onions.

CHAPTER SEVEN

Sauces and Dips

Hollandaise sauce

▲△△

GLUTEN-FREE   NUT-FREE   VEGETARIAN

PREP TIME: 5 minutes / **TOTAL TIME:** 5 minutes

SERVES: 4

Hollandaise is a beautiful pale yellow and has just a bit of tang from the lemon. This sauce is a cinch to whip up and makes a great sidekick to asparagus, broccoli, corn, or cabbage. You can also serve it as the star attraction on eggs Benedict.

2 egg yolks

½ cup melted butter, divided

1 tablespoon freshly squeezed lemon juice

½ teaspoon salt

Dash cayenne pepper

In a medium mixing bowl, with an electric hand mixer at high speed or by hand, beat the egg yolks for about 3 minutes, until thick and lemon-colored. Add 3 tablespoons of the melted butter, a little at a time, and beat constantly. Slowly beat in the remaining butter, alternating with the lemon juice. Add the salt and cayenne pepper and beat until combined.

HELPFUL HINT: If you have leftover sauce, cover and store it in the refrigerator for up to two days. To reheat it, place the bowl of sauce over lukewarm (not hot) water and stir it until the sauce returns to your desired consistency.

steak sauce

▲△△

PREP TIME: 5 minutes / **TOTAL TIME:** 5 minutes

SERVES: 6

You'll find so many uses for this steak sauce. It makes a great topping for grilled or broiled steaks, but it can also be mixed into ground beef to make hamburgers or meatloaf. My kids will even tell you it's the ultimate dipping sauce for French fries.

1 cup melted butter or vegetable oil

3 tablespoons ketchup

1 tablespoon Worcestershire sauce

2 teaspoons dry mustard

1½ tablespoons freshly squeezed lemon juice

In a small mixing bowl, combine the butter, ketchup, Worcestershire sauce, mustard, and lemon juice until well blended.

PRO TIP: If you're making this ahead of time, allow the sauce to warm to room temperature before using it.

Mustard Sauce

▲△△

EXTRA QUICK   NUT-FREE

PREP TIME: 5 minutes / **COOK TIME:** 10 minutes / **TOTAL TIME:** 15 minutes
MAKES: 1¼ cups

This mustard sauce tastes great on baked ham and other meats or on hearty vegetables like cabbage. It's also a delicious sandwich spread. You can add a quarter teaspoon of honey to the finished sauce for a terrific dip for chicken nuggets.

1 tablespoon melted butter

2 tablespoons all-purpose flour

1 cup boiling water

2 beef bouillon cubes

3 tablespoons prepared mustard

1 tablespoon Worcestershire sauce

1. In a medium saucepan over medium-high heat, whisk the butter and flour for about 2 minutes, until well blended and beginning to thicken into a roux.

2. Whisk the boiling water into your roux until it's smooth, then add the bouillon cubes and stir for about 4 minutes, until they dissolve. The sauce will begin to thicken. Add the prepared mustard and Worcestershire sauce. Remove from the heat and serve hot or cold.

JAZZ IT UP: Add one tablespoon of honey mustard sauce. You may want to add more honey, depending on the flavor you're looking for.

caramel sauce

▲△△

EXTRA QUICK   GLUTEN-FREE   NUT-FREE   VEGETARIAN

PREP TIME: 3 minutes / **COOK TIME:** 7 minutes / **TOTAL TIME:** 10 minutes
MAKES: about 1 cup

I love the simplicity of this caramel sauce. It's easy to make and complements so many dishes and desserts. If you want a richer caramel, substitute heavy (whipping) cream for the half-and-half. Dark sugar will give you a darker caramel and alter the flavor slightly. This caramel sauce goes well with pie, ice cream, and even some savory dishes like my Green Apple and Caramel Cheese Melt (page 87).

1 cup light brown
   sugar, packed

4 tablespoons
   unsalted butter

½ cup half-and-half

1 tablespoon vanilla extract

1 teaspoon sea
   salt (optional)

In a small saucepan over low heat, combine the brown sugar, butter, half-and-half, vanilla extract, and salt (if using) and bring the mixture to a simmer, whisking constantly, for about 7 minutes. The mixture will thicken as you stir. Keep in mind that once it's cooked, the sauce will thicken as it cools. Serve warm, at room temperature, or chilled from the fridge.

HELPFUL HINT: You can store leftover caramel sauce in an airtight container in the refrigerator for up to two weeks. Warm it on the stovetop or in a microwave before drizzling it over desserts.

Cheese sauce

▲△△

EXTRA QUICK   GLUTEN-FREE   NUT-FREE   VEGETARIAN

PREP TIME: 5 minutes / **COOK TIME:** 5 minutes / **TOTAL TIME:** 10 minutes
MAKES: 2 cups

This cheese sauce is perfect for dipping. You can drizzle it over nachos or cheese fries, serve it with tacos and enchiladas, or use it as a topping for hash browns or baked potatoes. There are so many possibilities.

1 cup mild cheddar cheese

¼ cup Monterey Jack cheese

4 ounces cream cheese

¼ cup milk

In a medium pot over low to medium heat, combine the cheddar, Monterey Jack, and cream cheeses. As the cheeses begin to melt, gradually stir in the milk. If you want a thinner cheese sauce, whisk in more milk.

PRO TIP: This Cheese Sauce will separate as it cools down. You can easily whisk it again to recombine it.

Chocolate Barbecue Sauce

▲△△

EXTRA QUICK   GLUTEN-FREE   NUT-FREE   VEGETARIAN

PREP TIME: 5 minutes / **COOK TIME:** 10 minutes / **TOTAL TIME:** 15 minutes
MAKES: about 2 cups

This barbecue sauce is excellent for dipping cookies, berries, or marshmallows to give them a chocolate coating with a bit of a kick. Just dip the fruit or cookies and let them rest on a lined baking sheet until the sauce sets. This sauce also makes a great glaze for my Baked Chicken Wings (page 51).

8 ounces 61% or 72% dark
   chocolate, chopped

1 tablespoon light
   corn syrup

1 cup heavy
   (whipping) cream

½ cup milk

4 tablespoons
   barbecue sauce

½ teaspoon hot sauce

1. Place the chocolate and corn syrup in a medium mixing bowl and set aside.

2. In a small saucepan over medium-high heat, pour in the cream and milk and bring it to a boil for about 8 minutes. Pour the hot cream and milk mixture over the chocolate in the bowl, whisking until the chocolate melts and the mixture is smooth.

3. Over a medium bowl, strain the mixture through a cheesecloth or fine mesh strainer. Add the barbecue sauce and hot sauce to the chocolate mixture and stir to combine.

SUB IN: Try using a quarter teaspoon of cayenne pepper in place of the hot sauce.

Carolina Barbecue Sauce

▲△△

DAIRY-FREE EXTRA QUICK GLUTEN-FREE NUT-FREE VEGETARIAN

PREP TIME: 5 minutes / **COOK TIME:** 15 minutes / **TOTAL TIME:** 20 minutes
MAKES: about 2½ cups

The Carolinas are known for their barbecue sauces. You'll find either thin, vinegar-based sauces or darker, thicker sauces made with ketchup. My take on a Carolina barbecue sauce combines both styles, with a bit of brown sugar and mustard added in to give it complex flavors. It's delicious on shredded pork, wings, and burgers. It's good stuff. Experiment with different types of vinegar for new flavors.

1 tablespoon extra-virgin olive oil

1 small onion, diced

1 cup vinegar

¾ cup ketchup

⅓ cup light brown sugar, packed

2 tablespoons spicy brown mustard

Heat the oil in a large saucepan over medium heat. Add the onion and cook for 5 minutes, until it begins to turn translucent. Stir in the vinegar, ketchup, brown sugar, and mustard. Once the sauce comes to a boil, reduce the heat and simmer for 5 minutes.

PRO TIP: You can use dark brown sugar if that's what you have. It will give the sauce a slightly different color and a new, delicious flavor.

Homemade Mayonnaise

▲▲△

EXTRA QUICK   GLUTEN-FREE   NUT-FREE   VEGETARIAN

PREP TIME: 5 minutes / **TOTAL TIME:** 5 minutes

MAKES: about 1½ cups

The flavor of this homemade mayonnaise is far superior to the store-bought kind, and it takes very little time to whip up. You'll want to put this creamy, tangy mayonnaise on everything. A food processor works best, but you can use an electric hand mixer with success.

1 large egg at
    room temperature

1 tablespoon
    English mustard

1 tablespoon white
    wine vinegar

1 cup canola or
    vegetable oil

¼ teaspoon salt

1 teaspoon freshly
    squeezed lemon
    juice (optional)

In the food processor or a small bowl, add the egg and begin mixing. Add the mustard and process for about 30 seconds, until a pale yellow. Add the vinegar. While still processing, begin slowly pouring in the oil until the mixture begins to thicken. Add the salt. Add the lemon juice, if using, and process for 5 seconds to combine.

PRO TIP: As a neutral oil, canola oil will give you the purest flavor, but you can also successfully use extra-virgin olive oil for a different spin.

Grandma Jana's Chili Sauce

▲▲△

DAIRY-FREE GLUTEN-FREE NUT-FREE VEGETARIAN

PREP TIME: 15 minutes / **COOK TIME:** 1 hour 40 minutes /
TOTAL TIME: 1 hour 55 minutes
MAKES: 3 pints

My Grandma Jana had a beautiful room filled with colorful jars of food she made and preserved. One of my favorites was her chili sauce, which is sweeter than salsa and seems to go with everything. You'll love it on Sunday mornings over hash browns or eggs and after school as a dipping sauce for tortilla chips. You can also try tucking this sauce into tacos or quesadillas, or baking chicken breasts covered with this sauce for a delicious entrée.

8 cups (about 12) tomatoes, chopped

1 green bell pepper, chopped

1 onion, chopped

½ cup sugar

1 tablespoon salt

½ teaspoon freshly ground black pepper

1 teaspoon cinnamon

1 teaspoon ground cloves

½ teaspoon allspice

1 teaspoon nutmeg

1 cup mild vinegar, like rice or balsamic

In a large saucepan over medium-low heat, cook the tomatoes for 1 hour, until they are a deep color and tender. Add the green bell pepper and onion and cook for 30 minutes. Stir in the sugar, salt, pepper, cinnamon, cloves, allspice, nutmeg, and vinegar. Increase the heat to medium-high and bring to a full, rolling boil. Boil for 10 minutes and stir, until the sauce is thick and the sugar is dissolved.

PRO TIP: White vinegar works here, but I prefer more mild vinegars. My favorite is rice vinegar, which has a mild flavor and melds wonderfully with the other flavors in this sauce.

Salsa Lizano

▲▲△

DAIRY-FREE **EXTRA QUICK** **GLUTEN-FREE** **NUT-FREE** **VEGETARIAN**

PREP TIME: 10 minutes / **COOK TIME:** 15 minutes / **TOTAL TIME:** 25 minutes
MAKES: 2 cups

This unique Costa Rican sauce is a tangy, sweet chile sauce with a very mild smoky flavor. It tastes delicious on eggs, rice, beans, or cheese, or as a marinade for poultry and beef.

1 cup water or
  vegetable stock

2 dried chiles, seeded

½ cup yellow
  onion, minced

1 carrot, minced

2 tablespoons sugar

2 tablespoons freshly
  squeezed lemon juice

1 tablespoon white
  wine vinegar

1 tablespoon cumin

2 teaspoons molasses

2 teaspoons freshly ground
  black pepper

2 teaspoons salt

½ teaspoon turmeric

½ teaspoon
  mustard powder

In a medium saucepan over medium heat, simmer the water and chiles for about 15 minutes, until the chiles are soft. Transfer the chile mixture into a blender. Add the onion, carrot, sugar, lemon juice, vinegar, cumin, molasses, pepper, salt, turmeric, and mustard and blend until smooth.

PRO TIP: This is an excellent sauce for all kinds of meats and poultry. Try it as a marinade for chicken, beef, and pork especially!

Homemade Pudding and Dirt Cups, page 165

CHAPTER EIGHT

Desserts

Easy Boston Cream Pie Cake

▲△△

EXTRA QUICK   NUT-FREE

PREP TIME: 5 minutes / **COOK TIME:** 1 minute / **TOTAL TIME:** 6 minutes
SERVES: 8 to 10

This might be the easiest dessert ever. It uses an angel food cake, sliced in half and filled with pudding, all topped with a premade container of chocolate frosting. It's so quick and easy, you'll want to make it every night of the week.

1 (1-ounce) box instant vanilla pudding

1½ cups cold milk

1 angel food cake, Bundt style

1 (16-ounce) tub premade chocolate frosting

1. In a small mixing bowl, mix the instant pudding with the cold milk for about 3 minutes, until thickened.

2. Slice the angel food cake horizontally into 3 even layers. Spread the pudding evenly over the three angel food cake layers, stacking each layer one after the other.

3. Heat the chocolate frosting in the microwave for 30 seconds in 10 second intervals, stirring after each cooking time. Stir the warmed frosting, and then pour it over the filled cake, letting it drip down the sides and over the edge of the center. Let the frosting rest for 5 minutes to set, and then serve.

JAZZ IT UP: Garnish this cake with slices of strawberry before the frosting sets for added color and tastiness.

Bread Pudding with Apples

▲△△

NUT-FREE (OPTIONAL) VEGETARIAN

PREP TIME: 15 minutes / **COOK TIME:** 45 minutes / **TOTAL TIME:** 1 hour
SERVES: 6 to 8

Bread pudding traces its origins all the way back to the eleventh century. For hundreds of years, people have been following this tradition to use up leftover or stale bread in a tasty dessert, though you can also use fresh bread. This is really good on its own or served with ice cream or whipped cream.

8 slices bread, cut into 1-inch cubes

¼ cup butter

1 cup hot milk

1 large apple, peeled, seeded, and cubed

½ cup raisins

½ cup granulated sugar

¼ teaspoon salt

½ teaspoon cinnamon

½ teaspoon nutmeg

2 eggs, beaten

½ cup chopped nuts (optional)

¾ cup brown sugar

1. Preheat the oven to 325°F. Butter a 1½-quart casserole dish.

2. Place the bread cubes in the prepared casserole dish so the bottom is covered. Melt the butter in the hot milk and pour it over the bread cubes. Set aside.

3. In a large mixing bowl, combine the apple, raisins, sugar, salt, cinnamon, and nutmeg. Toss to coat the fruit and combine the seasonings. Add the beaten eggs and nuts (if using), and then pour the mixture over the bread.

4. Bake on the center rack in the preheated oven for 45 minutes. The milk mixture should be fully absorbed into the bread when it's done.

JAZZ IT UP: Try experimenting with different types of bread, like cinnamon raisin bread, challah, or French bread. Each type of bread will yield a different taste and texture in your pudding.

popcorn Balls

▲ △ △

DAIRY-FREE   EXTRA QUICK   GLUTEN-FREE   NUT-FREE   VEGAN

PREP TIME: 10 minutes / **COOK TIME:** 10 minutes / **TOTAL TIME:** 20 minutes
MAKES: about 18 popcorn balls

These easy popcorn balls are a great snack. I love making them for family movie nights or when entertaining guests. They're also perfect for the holidays. You can dress them up for any occasion by rolling them in sprinkles or adding a drop or two of food coloring to the syrup.

Nonstick cooking spray

18 cups plain
    popped popcorn

2 cups sugar

1⅓ cups water

½ cup light corn syrup

1 teaspoon white vinegar

¼ teaspoon salt

1½ teaspoons
    vanilla extract

Dash candy
    flavoring (optional)

1. Line a large, flat surface with aluminum foil and spray it with nonstick cooking spray.

2. Spread the popcorn in a single layer on the prepared aluminum foil.

3. In a medium saucepan over high heat, combine the sugar, water, corn syrup, vinegar, and salt and cook for about 10 minutes, until the sugar dissolves and a candy thermometer inserted in the mixture reaches 255°F (hardball stage). Add the vanilla and candy flavoring, if using.

4. Pour the syrup mixture over the popcorn and stir gently with a spoon to coat. When the popcorn and syrup mixture is cool enough to handle, press the popcorn into 3-inch balls with lightly greased hands. Let cool completely on waxed paper.

JAZZ IT UP: Try adding mini marshmallows, pretzel pieces, or small chocolate candies to the popcorn when you spread it out.

Apple Spice Cake

▲△△

NUT-FREE VEGETARIAN

PREP TIME: 15 minutes / **COOK TIME:** 40 minutes / **TOTAL TIME:** 55 minutes
MAKES: 1 (13-by-9-inch) cake

This recipe is simple and quick, starting with a boxed cake mix and premade pie filling. You can make homemade frosting or use premade frosting as a shortcut. Either way, you'll add cinnamon to carry over the flavors from the cake. In less than an hour, you'll have a moist cake that people will ask you to make over and over.

Nonstick cooking spray

1 (21-ounce) can apple pie filling

1 box spice cake mix

¾ cup apple juice

⅓ cup vegetable oil

3 large eggs

1 container premade vanilla buttercream

½ teaspoon cinnamon

1. Preheat the oven to 350°F. Line a 9-by-13-inch pan with foil and spray it with nonstick cooking spray.

2. Open the can of pie filling and, while it's still in the can, dice the filling into small pieces with a sharp knife.

3. In a medium bowl, combine the cake mix, juice, oil, and eggs together until well blended. Slowly stir in the diced apple pie filling. Pour the batter into the prepared pan and bake for 40 minutes.

4. Let the cake cool completely before frosting. Remove the foil liner and lid from the frosting container and place it in the microwave for 10 seconds. Stir the frosting well and pour it over the cooled cake. Sprinkle the frosted cake with cinnamon. Let rest for 5 minutes for the frosting to set.

Peach and Berry Crisp

▲△△

NUT-FREE   VEGETARIAN

PREP TIME: 5 minutes / **COOK TIME:** 30 minutes / **TOTAL TIME:** 35 minutes
MAKES: 1 (8-by-8-inch) dessert

This crisp turns frozen peaches and berries into a warm dessert with a crumbly, lightly spiced topping in less than an hour. Serve it as is or add a scoop of vanilla ice cream, a dollop of whipped cream, or a drizzle of my Caramel Sauce (page 147).

1 (16-ounce) bag frozen peaches

1 (16-ounce) bag frozen berries (such as blackberries, strawberries, or blueberries)

⅔ cup brown sugar

½ cup flour

½ cup quick oats

1½ teaspoons cinnamon

1 teaspoon nutmeg

1 teaspoon allspice

⅓ cup light margarine

1. Preheat the oven to 375°F. Grease an 8-by-8-inch square pan.

2. Spread the frozen peaches and berries in the prepared pan.

3. In a medium mixing bowl, combine the brown sugar, flour, oats, cinnamon, nutmeg, and allspice. Cut the margarine into the mix with a fork until the mixture is crumbly and the pieces of margarine are about the size of peas. Sprinkle the topping over the fruit.

4. Bake on the center rack of the preheated oven for 30 to 35 minutes, until the topping is golden brown and the fruit is tender.

JAZZ IT UP: Serve this dessert with vanilla ice cream while the crisp is still warm.

Caramel Apple Tart

▲△△

EXTRA QUICK NUT-FREE VEGETARIAN

PREP TIME: 5 minutes / **COOK TIME:** 35 minutes / **TOTAL TIME:** 40 minutes
SERVES: 4

This easy caramel apple tart is made of flakey puff pastry topped with ooey-gooey caramel-coated apples and the perfect amount of cinnamon. It makes a special breakfast or delicious dessert.

1 sheet frozen ready-to-bake puff pastry, defrosted

5 medium Granny Smith apples, peeled and cored

2 tablespoons butter

16 pieces baking caramels, unwrapped

½ teaspoon ground cinnamon

1. Preheat the oven to 425°F. Line a sheet pan with parchment paper.

2. Place the puff pastry on the prepared pan. Using a rolling pin, slightly flatten the pastry and remove any creases. Prick the pastry surface all over with a fork. Bake it for 15 minutes, or until golden brown. Set aside.

3. Cut each apple into 8 wedges. In a large skillet over medium heat, melt the butter. Add the apples and cook for 10 minutes, stirring occasionally, until the apples begin to soften. Reduce the heat to low and cook for an additional 5 minutes, or until the apples are soft and cooked through. Transfer the apples to a plate and set aside.

4. Return the skillet to the burner over low heat. Add the baking caramels and cinnamon and cook for 5 minutes, stirring frequently. Return the apples to the skillet and fold them into the melted caramel. Spoon the apples and caramel over the pastry and serve.

SUB IN: For fuller flavor, you can use apple pie spice in place of the cinnamon.

Quick Sticky Buns

▲▲△

VEGETARIAN

PREP TIME: 1 hour / **COOK TIME:** 20 minutes / **TOTAL TIME:** 1 hour 20 minutes
MAKES: 8 buns

I love these sticky buns on Sunday mornings or holidays. They take a little over an hour, but the majority of the prep time is waiting for the dough to rise to make full, fluffy buns. These are best served warm, but they're still delightful once cooled completely.

2½ tablespoons
   unsalted butter

½ cup packed light brown
   sugar, divided

2 tablespoons light
   corn syrup

2 teaspoons freshly
   squeezed lemon juice

½ cup coarsely
   chopped pecans

1 (8-ounce) can
   refrigerated
   crescent dough

¾ teaspoon
   ground cinnamon

1. Preheat the oven to 375°F. Butter a 9-by-3-inch cake pan.

2. In a small saucepan over low heat, melt the butter. Whisk in ¼ cup of the brown sugar, then add the corn syrup and lemon juice and whisk until blended. Increase the heat to medium and whisk the mixture until the sugar melts. Bring to a slow, rolling boil for 2 minutes. Pour the syrup evenly over the bottom of the prepared cake pan. Sprinkle with the pecans.

3. Unroll the dough on a floured surface; press the perforations together. Roll out the dough into an 8-by-12-inch rectangle. Sprinkle it with the remaining ¼ cup of brown sugar and the cinnamon. Starting at the short side of the dough rectangle, roll up the dough. Cut the rolled-up dough crosswise into 8 (1-inch thick) rounds. Arrange the dough rounds, cut side down, in the pan with the syrup, spacing them evenly. Cover the pan with plastic wrap. Set it aside in a warm, draft-free area (a closed oven works great) to rise for about 45 minutes, until doubled in size.

4. Bake the buns in the preheated oven for about 20 minutes, until golden brown. Let them cool in the pan for 1 minute. Place a plate over the pan, invert the buns onto the plate, and lift the pan from the buns. Spoon any syrup remaining in the pan onto the buns and serve.

PRO TIP: Line your cake pan with parchment paper before adding the syrup and dough rounds for easier cleanup.

Chocolate Coconut Bars

▲▲△

DAIRY-FREE GLUTEN-FREE NUT-FREE VEGETARIAN

PREP TIME: 10 minutes / **COOK TIME:** 25 minutes / **TOTAL TIME:** 35 minutes
MAKES: 16 bars

These sweet yet hearty bars use coconut flour to make them gluten-free. They have an indulgent chocolate flavor that's complemented by coconut. These bars make a filling breakfast and can also be a good choice for dessert or a snack.

1½ cups coconut flour

1¼ cups quick-cooking rolled oats

¾ cup coconut sugar

½ cup unsweetened dark cocoa

2 teaspoons baking soda

1 teaspoon cinnamon

1 teaspoon salt

½ teaspoon baking powder

½ cup dark chocolate chips

3 large eggs

½ cup coconut butter/manna

½ cup coconut oil

1 teaspoon vanilla extract

¾ cup water (if too dry)

1. Preheat the oven to 350°F. Grease a 13-by-9-inch pan.

2. In a large mixing bowl, combine the coconut flour, rolled oats, coconut sugar, cocoa, baking soda, cinnamon, salt, and baking powder and stir until well mixed. Fold in the chocolate chips.

3. In a small bowl, combine the eggs, coconut butter/manna, coconut oil, and vanilla. Using a hand mixer, or by hand, beat the mixture until well combined. Add it to the dry ingredients and mix well. If the mixture is too dry (very thin and clumping) slowly add enough water to make it moist and able to be stirred, until it's about the consistency of brownie batter. Pour the mixture into the prepared pan and press it into the corners.

4. Bake on the center rack in the preheated oven for 25 to 30 minutes. Let it cool, and then cut it into bars.

JAZZ IT UP: When you remove the bars from the oven, sprinkle 1 cup of semi-sweet chocolate chips over the top. Allow them to sit for 2 minutes to melt, and then use a knife to spread the chocolate over the top of the bars for a layer of chocolate "frosting."

Homemade Pudding and Dirt Cups

▲▲△

VEGETARIAN

PREP TIME: 10 minutes / **COOK TIME:** 15 minutes / **TOTAL TIME:** 25 minutes
SERVES: 6

This recipe is the foundation for my favorite homemade pudding. Once you have the pudding ready, you can layer up some dirt cups for a fun dessert.

FOR THE PUDDING

4 tablespoons cornstarch

1½ cups sugar

4 cups milk

3 egg yolks

1 teaspoon vanilla extract

3 teaspoons butter

FOR THE DIRT CUPS

1 (16-ounce) package chocolate sandwich cookies

6 (8-ounce) cups, for serving

6 gummy worms

1 (6.5-ounce) can whipped cream

TO MAKE THE PUDDING

1. In a medium saucepan over medium heat, combine the cornstarch and the sugar. Whisk the mixture to get any lumps out. Slowly add the milk and cook for 5 minutes, or until the sugar dissolves. Add the egg yolks before the mixture gets too hot and stir for about 5 minutes, until thickened. Remove from the heat. Add the vanilla and butter, along with any flavor additions, and whisk until smooth.

TO MAKE THE DIRT CUPS

2. While the pudding cools, place the sandwich cookies in a resealable bag and crush them into fine crumbs with a rolling pin. Pour 1 tablespoon of the cookie crumbs into the bottom of each cup. Spoon the warm pudding into the cups. Add the remaining cookie crumbs to the top of each cup and stick one gummy worm in the "dirt," draping the end of the gummy over the cup. Top each cup with whipped cream and enjoy!

> **SUB IN:** For chocolate pudding, add four tablespoons of cocoa powder.

Cranberry and Pistachio Biscotti

▲▲△

DAIRY-FREE   VEGETARIAN

PREP TIME: 15 minutes / **COOK TIME:** 45 minutes / **TOTAL TIME:** 1 hour
MAKES: about 24 to 32 biscotti

Biscotti is a hard, cookie-like biscuit. The word means "twice cooked," which is how this recipe works. You'll bake the dough, cut it into the biscuits, and then bake them again at a lower temperature to dry them out and increase their shelf life. These are excellent dipped in milk, hot chocolate, coffee, or tea.

¼ cup extra-virgin olive oil

¾ cup sugar

2 teaspoons vanilla extract

½ teaspoon almond extract

2 large eggs

1¾ cups flour

1 teaspoon baking powder

¼ teaspoon salt

1½ cups unsalted, shelled pistachios (if they are salted, omit the salt from the recipe)

¾ cup dried cranberries

1. Preheat the oven to 300°F. Grease a cookie sheet.

2. In a small bowl, blend the olive oil and sugar with an electric mixer. Add the vanilla, almond extract, and eggs, beating the mixture until blended.

3. In a separate small bowl, combine the flour, baking powder, and salt and whisk together until mixed. At low speed, gradually add the dry ingredients to the egg mixture. Mix in the pistachios and cranberries by hand and divide the dough in half.

4. On the prepared cookie sheet, form each dough half into a 12-by-2-inch log. Space the logs about 4 inches apart (the dough may be sticky; use cold water on your hands if necessary).

5. Bake in the preheated oven for 35 minutes, or until the logs are light brown. Remove them from oven and reduce the oven's temperature to 275°F. Let the logs cool for about 10 minutes. Using a sharp knife, cut each log diagonally to form cookies about ¾ inches wide. Lay them on their sides on the cookie sheet and return them to the oven for 8 to 10 minutes.

Molten Caramel Cakes

▲▲△

NUT-FREE   VEGETARIAN

PREP TIME: 15 minutes / **COOK TIME:** 30 minutes / **TOTAL TIME:** 45 minutes
MAKES: 6 (6-ounce) cakes

These mini chocolate cakes are a delight to eat. You serve them warm, and as soon as you cut into one, a ribbon of caramel flows out. I recommend making them with my homemade Caramel Sauce (page 147); the taste is worth the extra effort.

Nonstick cooking spray

1 box chocolate cake mix

6 tablespoons caramel sauce

1. Preheat the oven to 350°F. Spray six small ramekins with nonstick cooking spray. Place a roasting pan in the oven and fill it with ½ inch of hot water.

2. In a large bowl, prepare the cake batter according to the package directions. Spoon half of the batter into the ramekins. Drop 1 tablespoon of the caramel sauce into the center of each ramekin. Cover them evenly with the remaining batter. Place the ramekins in the prepared roasting pan.

3. Bake in the preheated oven for about 30 minutes, or until the cakes have cracks on their tops and have risen. Let them cool for 5 minutes, then serve warm.

PRO TIP: Do not open the oven while the cakes are baking. Look through the oven window; you can turn on the oven light, too, if it's difficult to see.

snickerdoodles

▲▲△

PREP TIME: 15 minutes / **COOK TIME:** 15 minutes / **TOTAL TIME:** 30 minutes
MAKES: 36 large cookies

These might just be my favorite cookies. The dough is rolled in cinnamon sugar before baking, giving these cookies a burst of cinnamon flavor in every bite.

3¾ cups all-purpose flour

2 teaspoons
    ground cinnamon

1 teaspoon baking powder

¼ teaspoon cream of tartar

2 cups sugar

1 cup butter, softened

2 eggs

¼ cup milk

1 teaspoon vanilla extract

3 tablespoons
    cinnamon sugar

1. Preheat the oven to 375°F.

2. In a medium mixing bowl, combine the flour, cinnamon, baking powder, and cream of tartar and stir to mix well.

3. In a large mixing bowl, add the sugar and butter and beat with an electric hand mixer on high speed until fluffy. Add the eggs, milk, and vanilla and beat on low until combined.

4. Slowly add the flour mixture to the butter mixture, beating on low until combined (you can refrigerate the dough for 1 hour at this point to make it easier to work with, but it is not required).

5. Use your hands to form the cookie dough into golf ball-size balls. Roll each ball in the cinnamon sugar and place them on an ungreased cookie sheet. Flatten the cookies with the bottom of a glass. Bake on the center rack of the preheated oven for 11 to 14 minutes, or until golden brown. Remove from the pan and let cool.

Salted Caramel Pear Pie

▲▲▲

NUT-FREE   VEGETARIAN

PREP TIME: 15 minutes / **COOK TIME:** 55 minutes / **TOTAL TIME:** 1 hour 10 minutes
MAKES: 1 (9-inch) pie

This impressive pie is a tasty combination of caramel and baked pears. I recommend making it with my Caramel Sauce for the best flavor, though you can also use a store-bought sauce as a shortcut if you must.

1 (2-count, 14-ounce) box
   refrigerated pie crusts

6 pears, peeled and cut into
   ½-inch pieces

¼ cup sugar, plus extra
   for sprinkling

¼ cup all-purpose flour

1 teaspoon
   ground cinnamon

1 tablespoon freshly
   squeezed lemon juice

1 cup salted Caramel Sauce
   (page 147), divided

1 large egg

1 tablespoon milk

1. Preheat the oven to 400°F.

2. Divide the box of pie crusts in half for one top crust and one bottom crust. Roll out one pie crust to a 12-inch circle using the directions on the box. Carefully place it in the bottom of a 9-by-2-inch pie dish. Make sure it is smooth.

3. In a medium mixing bowl, combine the pears, sugar, flour, cinnamon, and lemon juice. Stir until the pears are well coated. Spoon the filling into the pie dish, discarding any excess liquid in the bowl (the liquid will make your pie soggy). Drizzle ½ cup of the caramel sauce evenly across the top. Cover the pie dish with plastic wrap and place it in the refrigerator while you make the top crust.

4. Using the other half of the prepared pie crust, follow the package directions to roll it out and place it on top of the pie. Use a fork or sharp knife to prick holes in the top crust to allow ventilation. Beat the egg with the milk to create an egg wash. Lightly brush the top of the pie crust with the egg wash and sprinkle the brushed crust with sugar.

CONTINUED >

5. Place the pie on a large baking sheet. Bake on the center rack of the preheated oven for 20 minutes. Then, use a pie crust shield or place strips of aluminum foil over the edges of the pie crust to prevent them from burning. Reduce the temperature to 350°F and bake for an additional 35 minutes, or until the pie crust is golden brown.

6. Allow the pie to cool for 3 hours at room temperature before serving. Drizzle the slices of pie with the remaining caramel sauce and serve.

PRO TIP: For the best results, use a spoon and a level to more accurately measure the flour. Scooping it up directly in a measuring cup can pack more flour in than the recipe calls for.

MEASUREMENT CONVERSIONS

Volume Equivalents (Liquid)

US STANDARD	US STANDARD (OUNCES)	METRIC (APPROXIMATE)
2 tablespoons	1 fl. oz.	30 mL
¼ cup	2 fl. oz.	60 mL
½ cup	4 fl. oz.	120 mL
1 cup	8 fl. oz.	240 mL
1½ cups	12 fl. oz.	355 mL
2 cups or 1 pint	16 fl. oz.	475 mL
4 cups or 1 quart	32 fl. oz.	1 L
1 gallon	128 fl. oz.	4 L

Oven Temperatures

FAHRENHEIT (F)	CELSIUS (C) (APPROXIMATE)
250°	120°
300°	150°
325°	165°
350°	180°
375°	190°
400°	200°
425°	220°
450°	230°

Volume Equivalents (Dry)

US STANDARD	METRIC (APPROXIMATE)
⅛ teaspoon	0.5 mL
¼ teaspoon	1 mL
½ teaspoon	2 mL
¾ teaspoon	4 mL
1 teaspoon	5 mL
1 tablespoon	15 mL
¼ cup	59 mL
⅓ cup	79 mL
½ cup	118 mL
⅔ cup	156 mL
¾ cup	177 mL
1 cup	235 mL
2 cups or 1 pint	475 mL
3 cups	700 mL
4 cups or 1 quart	1 L

Weight Equivalents

US STANDARD	METRIC (APPROXIMATE)
½ ounce	15 g
1 ounce	30 g
2 ounces	60 g
4 ounces	115 g
8 ounces	225 g
12 ounces	340 g
16 ounces or 1 pound	455 g

INDEX

ACKNOWLEDGMENTS

I would like to extend the most gracious thank you to the following people:

Mitzi, for keeping me on task with my deadlines and just being the best friend.

Alexis, for helping me with techniques and making me laugh when the stress was high.

Sherri, for all your work in helping me type and format the recipes. I am especially grateful that we share such a love for recipes, and for learning more about your mom.

Finally, a shout-out to my family, who adapted their schedules to accommodate mine and gave feedback on my cooking.

I love you all.

ABOUT THE AUTHOR

Julee Morrison is a blogger and a mother of six who lives in the foothills of Virginia with two dogs. Her first book, *The Instant Pot® College Cookbook: 75 Quick and Easy Meals that Taste Like Home*, celebrates her family recipes and helps readers make quick meals everyone will love. Her most recent book, *The How-To Cookbook for Teens: 100 Easy Recipes to Learn the Basics*, gets teens into the kitchen for the first time.

NOTES

NOTES

NOTES

NOTES

NOTES

NOTES

NOTES

NOTES